KERNEL OF THE KERNEL

SUNY Series in Islam

Seyyed Hossein Nasr, editor

Kernel of the Kernel

Concerning the Wayfaring and Spiritual Journey of the People of Intellect

(Risāla-yi Lubb al-Lubāb dar Sayr wa Sulūk-i Ulu'l Albāb)

A Shīʿī Approach to Sufism

From the Teachings of
SAYYID MUḤAMMAD ḤUSAYN ṬABĀṬABĀ'Ī

Compiled, Edited, and Expanded by
SAYYID MUḤAMMAD ḤUSAYN ḤUSAYNĪ TIHRĀNĪ

Translated by
MOHAMMAD H. FAGHFOORY

Foreword by
Seyyed Hossein Nasr

State University of New York Press

Published by
State University of New York Press, Albany

Printed in the United States of America

For information, address State University of New York Press,
90 State Street, Suite 700, Albany, NY 12207

Production by Dana Foote
Marketing by Anne M. Valentine

Library of Congress Cataloging-in-Publication Data

Ḥusaynī Tihrānī, Muhammad Husayn.
[Risālah-'i Lubb al-lubāb. English]
Kernel of the kernel : Risāla-yi Lubb al-lubāb dar sayr wa sulūk-i ulu'l albāb [sic] / [based on lectures] by Sayyid Muḥammad Ḥusayn Tabātabā'ī ; compiled, expanded, and edited by Sayyid Muhammad Ḥusayn Ḥusaynī Tihrānī ; translated by Mohammad H. Faghfoory ; preface by Seyyed Hossein Nasr.
p. cm.
Includes bibliographical references and index.
ISBN 0-7914-5237-9 (alk. paper)— ISBN 0-7914-5238-7 (pbk. : alk. paper)
1. Religious life—Islam—Koranic teaching. 2. Religious life—Shī'ah. 3. God (Islam)—Koranic teaching. 4. Islam—Essence, genius, nature. 5. Sufism. I. Title: Risāla-yi Lubb al-lubāb dar sayr wa sulūk-i ulu'l albāb [sic]. II. Tabātabā'ī, Muḥammad Ḥusayn. III. Faghfoory, Mohammad Hassan. IV. Title.
BP132 .H88613 2003
297.4—dc 21 2002021109

10 9 8 7 6 5 4 3 2 1

Humbly dedicated in gratitude to the blessed memories
of ʿAllāmah Sayyid Muḥammad Ḥusayn Ṭabāṭabāʾī and
ʿAllāmah Sayyid Muḥammad Ḥusayn Ḥusaynī Tihrānī
May God's Mercy be upon their immaculate souls
and to
Shaykh al-Sayyid al-Ḥusayn al-Shādhilī
who awakens hearts to His call
with Silent Music

CONTENTS

FOREWORD

Seyyed Hossein Nasr

The work of 'Allāmah Ṭihrānī translated here represents a genre of Islamic gnostic and esoteric writings that has been rarely studied in the West until now. This book is in fact perhaps the first of its kind to appear in the English language. In order to understand what intellectual strand this work represents, it is necessary to delve in a general way into the different manifestations of Islamic esoteric teachings. The first and best-known crystallization of the inner or esoteric teachings of the Islamic revelation is of course Sufism, which has produced a vast treasury of writings ranging from practical advice to the lives of saints, from ethical treatises to poetry and from short aphorism and letters to didactic works dealing with Islamic metaphysics, cosmology, psychology, and eschatology along with a number of other subjects. This latter category of writings is associated especially with the intellectual teachings of Sufism, dealing as it does with unitive knowledge known as gnosis or *'irfān/ma'rifah.* Its greatest expositor was Ibn 'Arabī many of whose works as well as those belonging to his school have now been translated and studied in many European languages, especially English and French.

A second crystallization of Islamic esoteric teachings is to be found in Ismā'īlī philosophical and theological writings which, despite their special color associated with a particular branch of Shī'ism, contain many teachings drawn also from the universal sources of Islamic esoterism. In fact historically Ismā'īlism was close to Sufism both in its origin and during its later history after the Mongol invasion when at least in Persia Ismā'īlism appeared often in the dress of Sufism and there appeared Ismā'īlī commentaries to well known Sufi works. During the Qājār period some of the Ismā'īlī Imāms even received Sufi initiation. This category of writings is also known in the West and many translations and studies of Ismā'īlī doctrinal works have appeared in various European languages over the years.

A third category is Twelve-Imāmī Shī'ite gnosis *('irfān-i shī'ī)*, which has produced a vast body of works many, but not exclusively, in Persian, by such figures as Sayyid Ḥaydar Āmulī, Ibn Turkah, Fayḍ Kāshānī, and Qāḍī Sa'īd Qummī, not to speak of mystical philosophers and theosophers who combined philosophy and gnosis, such as Mullā Ṣadrā and his followers during the past few centuries and down to our day, including Ḥājjī Mullā Hādī Sabzawārī, who lived in the Qājār period, as well as many of the philosopher-gnostics of the present century. In fact, as far as Persia is concerned, the School of Tehran founded at the end of the eighteenth century, with the advent of the Qājārs, possessed two branches from the beginning: one devoted to philosophy especially of the School of Mullā Ṣadrā and the second to pure Islamic esoterism in the form of gnosis. This latter school was founded by Sayyid Raḍī Lārījānī who was given the title Mālik al-Bāṭin, the "Possessor of the Esoteric," and was the teacher of the most famous gnostic of the thirteenth/nineteenth century in Persia, Muḥammad Riḍā Qumsha'ī, called the Ibn 'Arabī of his day, who was followed by figures distinguished by their mastery of Ibn 'Arabian gnosis, and Islamic esoteric teaching in general, such as Mīrzā Naṣīr Gīlānī, Mīr Sayyid Shihāb al-Dīn Nayrīzī, Mīrzā Aḥmad Āshtiyānī, and three of my own most eminent teachers in the traditional sciences, Sayyid Muhammad Kāẓim 'Aṣṣār, Muḥyi al-Dīn Mahdī Ilāhī Qumsha'ī, and Sayyid Muhammad Ḥusayn Ṭabāṭabā'ī. The teachings of the latter figure constitutes the original material for this present work. To this list must also be added a number of figures well versed in *'irfān* but celebrated more in other domains, such as jurisprudence and politics, including Ayatollāh Khumaynī whose commentaries on the works of Ibn 'Arabī are well known in Persia and have now gained some fame in the West.

The writings of the figures in the field of gnosis cited here are not, for the most part, known in the West although they are now gaining some attention in the outside world, thanks to the efforts of Henry Corbin and a number of other scholars. In Persia, at least as a result of religio-political tensions between the later Ṣafavid religious scholars and the established Sufi orders, especially the Ni 'matallāhī, the term "Sufi" became anathema in Shī'ite religious circles and the term "gnosis" or *'irfān,* came to replace *taṣawwuf* in many contexts. While during earlier periods as leading a Shī'ite scholar as Sayyid Ḥaydar Āmulī identified himself openly with Sufism, from the latter part of the eleventh/seventeenth century onward the

Shīʿite *ʿulamāʾ* distanced themselves for the most part from ordinary Sufism, which they referred to as *taṣawwuf-i khānaqāhī* (literary Sufism associated with Sufi centers). Moreover, this parting of ways did not include only those exoteric *ʿulamāʾ* who were opposed to the esoteric as such but also those who were attracted to the esoteric and who were in fact inwardly totally immersed in the world of Sufi gnosis, associating themselves with the works of the great Sufi masters such as Ibn ʿArabī, Rūmī, and Jāmī.

The question arises concerning the source of esoteric knowledge of these men all of whom were pious and many of whom were saintly. Did their knowledge involve only theoretical learning? Were they led by the Hidden Imām and/or the mysterious Prophet Khaḍir? Did they have a human master and receive initiation and spiritual guidance as is the case with Sufism? These question have been debated a great deal concerning such famous figures as Mullā Ṣadrā, as well as others. I remember discussing this issue for years with Corbin concerning Mullā Ṣadrā. Corbin believed that he had no human teacher whereas I believed and still believe that he had a human teacher who initiated him into the knowledge of the Divine Mysteries *(asrār-i ilāhī)*.

In any case, most scholars dealing with the Shīʿite world believe that in addition to the Sufi orders, such as the Dhahabī and Niʿmatallāhī which are *khānaqāhī* and similar to the great Sufi orders in the Sunni world with their regular initiatic chain *(silsilah)* linking master to disciple over the centuries and reaching back to the origin of the Qurʾānic revelation, there is also the general esoteric aspect of Shīʿism that bestows a gnostic character on certain Shīʿite works as well as the presence of spiritual guidance by the Imāms, especially the Twelfth in the case of at least a number of figures possessing esoteric knowledge of the highest order.

What has not been studied seriously until now is the presence within Twelve-Imāmī Shīʿism of a fourth category, which includes those who belong to an initiatic chain linking master to disciple but without the formal organization that characterizes the well-known Sufi orders. This chain may be called a Sufi *silsilah,* without the name Sufi, but involving regular transmission of initiatic power, spiritual direction, spiritual practices and the like all resembling Sufism. Such lines of transmission were preserved in secret mostly among the class of Shīʿite *ʿulamāʾ* and are the reason for the appearance of a number of eminent gnostics and saints belonging to the *ʿulamāʾ* class. A somewhat similar situation may be said to exist in the Sunni world, for example, at al-Azhar University where there is a very secret branch of the Naqshbandiyyah Order tailored especially for the *'ulamā'* of that eminent Sunni center of learning.

This regular chain of transmission in Shī'ism was and remains very hidden. Its methods and disciplines are taught only orally and those who are its masters select a few among their usually large number of religious students to initiate them into this path of spiritual perfection parallel with teaching them the major texts of theoretical *'irfān.* In the various religious schools *(ḥawzahs)* of the Shī'ite world, whether it be in Persia, Iraq, Pakistan, India, or elsewhere a number of students advance enough to be accepted in classes in which the works of Ibn 'Arabī, Ṣadr al-Dīn Qunawī, and others are taught. But not all students who reach these levels; even those who study the most advanced texts, such as the *Miṣbāḥ al-uns* of al-Fanārī, are permitted into the inner circle of initiates. In order to receive initiation there is also the necessity of the presence in the being of the disciple of spiritual virtue, spiritual will *(himmah),* a deep yearning for the Divine and thirst for the realization of metaphysical knowledge.

The book of 'Allāmah Ṭihrānī is a fruit of this hidden tree of Islamic esoterism. Being itself a recension of the oral teachings of his master 'Allāmah Ṭabāṭabā'ī, the work is a fine example of the kind of writing which, in the context of Shī'ite traditions and commentaries upon the Qur'ān, discuss the stages of the spiritual path and reveal glimpses of that unitive knowledge that lies at the end of that path. An earlier example of such a work is the *Sayr wa sulūk* ("Spiritual Wayfaring") by the eminent Qājār religious scholar and authority on esoteric knowledge Baḥr al-'ulūm, who was also a master of this secret and hidden esoteric chain. 'Allāmah Ṭihrānī himself mentions his esoteric teachers whose chain can be summarized as in the chart that follows.

All these figures were eminent teachers in Persia and Iraq and respected highly as not only religious scholars, but also as saintly men to some of whom miracles were attributed. But only those who were initiated and guided inwardly by them became aware of their inner reality and were able to gain access to the treasury of Divine Mysteries whose keys they held. I studied for some twenty years with 'Allāmah Ṭabāṭabā'ī and became aware through him of the rigorous spiritual discipline that "their path" required and also of the inner reality of at least one of the masters of this "hidden *ṭarīqah.*" He once told me that he had studied the *Fuṣūṣ* of Ibn 'Arabī for years in Persia and thought that he knew this central work of Sufi gnosis

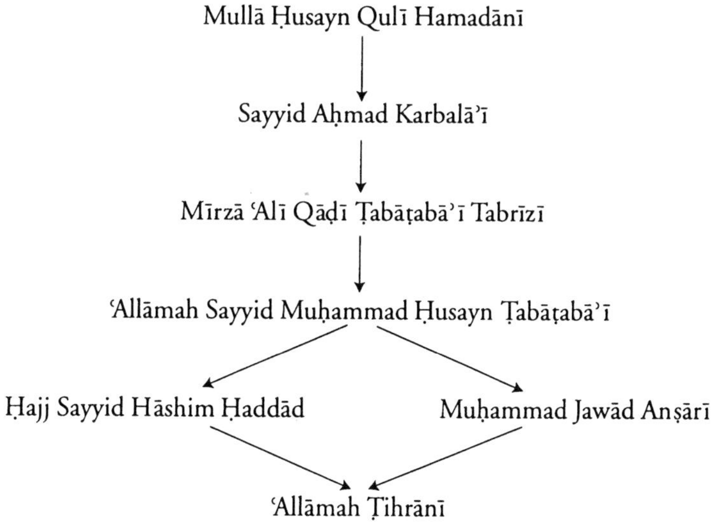

well before he set out to continue his studies in Najaf. Once in that city he decided to attend the private lessons being given by Mīrzā 'Alī Qāḍī on the *Fuṣūṣ*. The venerable and saintly 'Allāmah Ṭabāṭabā'ī told me that during the first hour of the course his whole state *(ḥāl)* began to change and he heard the walls of the room echoing Shaykh al-Akbar's words. He realized that until then he had only known the outward meaning of the words of the text and was only now beginning to understand what they *really* meant. The master later initiated the young 'Allāmah, who began to undergo, parallel with his formal studies, rigorous spiritual discipline with long fasts of silence that affected his presence for the rest of his life. One could not be in his presence, even when he was teaching, without experiencing something of the holy silence from which all words worthy of the name proceed and to which they all return.

While teaching at Qum for over thirty years, 'Allāmah Ṭabāṭabā'ī taught regular courses on Ibn Sīnā's *Shifā'* and Mullā Ṣadrā's *Asfār.* On weekends he taught a smaller number of students in a private gathering texts of *'irfān,* such as the works of Ibn 'Arabī and Ibn Turkah. Then he had an even more select circle of students who were initiated into the mysteries of gnosis and spiritual wayfaring. The book translated here is the recession of the teachings of 'Allāmah Ṭabāṭabā'ī in those most intimate gatherings compiled by 'Allāmah Ṭihrānī, who as a student in the 1940s and 1950s attended those sessions. The work represents therefore the more esoteric aspect of the teachings of 'Allāmah Ṭabāṭabā'ī whose other works on the Qur'ān, Shī'ism, and Islamic philosophy are well known, some already translated into English. This work in fact reveals the inner aspect of the teachings of one of the greatest Islamic scholars of the twentieth century and is also the first specimen of this kind of writing, belonging to the hidden initiatic line already mentioned, that has been rendered into English.

For historical reasons a word must also be said about Murtaḍā Muṭahharī, for whom 'Allāmah Ṭihrānī wrote the introduction to this work. Muṭahharī was one of the most gifted students of 'Allāmah Ṭabāṭabā'ī, and a close friend of mine with whom I participated in many intellectual and religious endeavors. He possessed a keen philosophical mind but was also an activist. 'Allāmah Ṭabāṭabā'ī wanted him to be less active outwardly and devote more time to serious philosophical studies and contemplation. Muṭahharī had written a commentary on the first three books of 'Allāmah Ṭabāṭabā'ī's *Uṣūl-i falsafa-yi ri'ālizm* ("The Principles of the Philosophy of Realism") but years had passed and he had not succeeded in finishing the commentary claiming always that he was too busy. One day when both of us were in his presence, 'Allāmah Ṭabāṭabā'ī turned to me without looking at Muṭahharī and said, "Please tell Āqā Murtaḍā [i.e., Muṭahharī] to make fewer speeches and devote more time to introspection and to finish the commentary." But the word of the master was to no avail and despite his closeness to his teacher, Muṭahharī showed little interest in a more contemplative life and in the master's esoteric teachings.

Early in the 1960s, however, he was arrested and imprisoned for a couple of months. Prisoners were allowed to ask for books and the first work that he asked his family to bring to him was the *Mathnawī* of Rūmī. Once out of prison, he told me how fruitful and calming that period had been and that an opening had been created in his soul for philosophical contemplation and particularly *'irfān* in both its aspect of theory *(naẓar)* and practice *('amal)*. Outwardly he continued to have an active life, which was to lead to direct political participation in the tumultuous events of 1978 and finally to his tragic assassination in 1979. But inwardly he continued to be drawn ever more to the esoteric tradition and the inner teachings of 'Allāmah Ṭabāṭabā'ī, summarized in this short but pithy work, the *Lubb al-lubāb*, which is truly the kernel of the kernel of the fruit of revelation and which is given a title that is also used by Ibn 'Arabī in one of his well-known works. Something of the inner transformation of the late Murtaḍā Muṭahharī is also present in this work and his spirit seems to have inspired his old friend 'Allāmah Ṭihrānī to compile the work in its present form.

Something also needs to be said in this preface about 'Allāmah Ṭihrānī himself. The publication of his complete works in recent years reveals his astonishing output in both quantity and diversity. His works range from those dealing with the Qur'ān, Imāmology, eschatology, and other theological issues to those concerned with the esoteric and mystical dimensions of Islam. In contrast to his teacher 'Allāmah Ṭabāṭabā'ī, who refused to write on current events and politics in the ordinary sense of the term, 'Allāmah Ṭihrānī also wrote on contingent problems posed in the early years of the Islamic Revolution in Iran, resulting in certain assertions that were to be challenged and opposed later by other religious authorities in Persia itself. This aspect of his work belongs precisely to the realm of contingency and is quite dated but it should not in any way cast a shadow on the vast body of traditional studies that he has left behind and that represents one of the most imposing bodies of scholarly works produced by a single author in the Islamic world during this century. Also the fact that 'Allāmah Ṭihrānī was so encyclopedic in the scope of his knowledge did not in any way detract from the depth of his scholarship and understanding. He exemplifies a case of a whole category of Islamic writers going back to Fārābī, Ibn Sīnā, and Naṣīr al-Dīn Ṭūsī, for whom extension of breadth did not mean in any sense the loss of depth.

Aside from its historical and theological significance, the *Lubb al-lubāb* or *Kernel of the Kernel* stands by itself as a masterpiece in the field of spirituality and gnosis. While naturally couched in the language and terminology of the Qur'ān and *Ḥadīth,* it conveys a message of a universal order meant for all human beings. It is a significant work not only because it makes known in the English language a hitherto unknown current of Islamic esoterism and gnosis. It is significant most of all because it deals with the deepest metaphysical and spiritual realities, which should attract all those persons, Muslims and non-Muslims alike, who are in quest of the spiritual treasures hidden within the inner teachings of revelation that also lie deep within that primordial human nature which, although now hidden and difficult of access to most men, still constitutes the very center of our being.

—Seyyed Hossein Nasr

TRANSLATOR'S INTRODUCTION

The text that is presented in the following pages is one of the most important books written on Sufism from an Iranian-Shīʿite point of view in the twentieth century. In a profound yet simple manner, the *Lubb al-Lubāb dar sayr wa sulūk-i ulu'l-albāb (Kernel of the Kernel Concerning the Wayfaring and Spiritual Journey of the People of Intellect)* discusses the stages and processes that an aspiring wayfarer must go through in order to attain spiritual realization. In addition, it illustrates the Qur'ānic origins of *ʿirfān* (gnosis) as well as its relationship with Shīʿism. Finally, the book demonstrates the meaning of the concept of *walāyat* (Arabic *Walāyah*) and the role of the Shīʿite Imāms in transmitting esoteric knowledge and truths about *tawḥīd* (Divine Unity), their part in the Shīʿites' spiritual life, and the place of the *Ahl al-Bayt* (Household) of the Blessed Prophet of Islam in the spiritual journey toward God.

The *Lubb al-Lubāb* is in fact a product of love and the labor of two scholars. Āyatullāh ʿAllāmah Sayyid Muhammad Ḥusayn Ṭabāṭabā'ī was one of the most prominent Iranian *ʿulamā* of the twentieth century and a professor of Islamic philosophy, jurisprudence, ethics, and gnosis in the *madrasahs* or seminaries of Qum for over thirty-seven years. He was an eminent religious scholar, an original thinker, a philosopher, a theosopher, a poet, a prolific writer, a commentator of the Qur'ān, and an exalted gnostic of great spiritual realization. His spiritual life as well as his scholarly achievements have been studied extensively in Persian and English in recent years and need no further introduction.[1]

The *Lubb al-Lubāb* was originally a series of lectures that the ʿAllāmah delivered to a select group of his students and disciples in Qum between 1368 A.H./1949 and 1369/1950. Āyatullāh Sayyid Muhammad Ḥusayn Tihrānī, who was then twenty-five years old and one of ʿAllāmah Ṭabāṭabā'ī's most brilliant students, took extensive notes while he lectured. A few years before his own death, Tihrānī, who had also earned the honorific title of *ʿAllāmah* (most learned), compiled, edited, and expanded the series and published it in its present form in Mashhad. The translation presented here is based on the seventh edition of the book that was published in 1417 A.H./1996 (1375 solar).[2]

Despite numerous contributions to the field of Islamic studies and considerable recognition and respect in the scholarly community in Qum and Mashhad, 'Allāmah Tihrānī has remained unknown outside Iran. As yet, no scholarly account of his life and thought has been produced in any language, including Persian. Therefore, it is appropriate to present a short biographical sketch of his life and briefly examine his religious thought and intellectual orientation.

Āyatullāh 'Allāmah Tihrānī is related to many prominent Shīʿī-Iranian *ʿulamā* of previous centuries by birth and/or marriage, including such notable scholars as Muhammad Bāqir Majlīsī, Āyatullāhs Mīrzā Muhammad Tihrānī, the author of *Mustadrik al-Biḥār,* Muhammad Ṣaliḥ Khātūnābādī, and Sayyid Mahdī Baḥr al-ʿUlūm.

According to available biographical information, 'Allāmah Tihrānī was born in Tehran in 1345 A.H./1925 (1303 solar) and passed away in Mashhad in 1416 A.H./1995 (1374 solar). His grandfather, Āyatullāh Ḥājj Sayyid Ibrāhim had studied in Najaf with Āyatullāh Mīrzā Ḥassan Shīrāzī (among the *ʿulamā* known as *Mīrzā-yi awwal*/first Mīrzā, d. 1312/1894). The 'Allāmah's father, Āyatullāh Sayyid Muhammad Ṣādiq, was a student of Mīrzā Muhammad Taqī Shīrāzī (known as *Mīrzā-yi duwwum*/second Mīrzā, d. 1339/1920). After completing his education in Samarra, Muhammad Ṣādiq returned to Iran and settled in Tehran. Little is written about Muhammad Ṣādiq's life and career during the reign of Riḍā Shāh (1925–1941). There is much evidence, however, which points to his active involvement in open oppositional activity against Riḍā Shāh's government. Several observers, including 'Allāmah Tihrānī himself, testify that like many other members of the clergy, Āyatullāh Muhammad Ṣādiq strongly opposed secularization and Westernization of Iran. He was particularly active in organizing and leading the government's opponents in Tehran against the law for unifiormity of dress introduced in December 1928/1307 (solar), and the law for the abolition of women's veil promulgated in 1935/1314 (solar). As a result of these activities Muhammad Ṣādiq was arrested and imprisoned several times. Despite the government's attempt to discredit him, he survived and remained one of the top-ranking and most respected *mujtahids* of Tehran in the early and middle decades of the twentieth century.[3]

Unlike his father, the young Muhammad Ḥusayn did not receive his early religious education in the theological schools of Qum or Tehran. He studied with his father at home until he became well versed in the Islamic sciences. He also received a modern education during the 1930s and 1940s in Tehran. After completing elementary school and three years of secondary school he entered the German Technical School in Tehran, and in 1942, graduated with a degree in mechanical engineering. It was only then in 1364 A.H./1943 (solar 1322) that Muhammad Ḥusayn entered the *Ḥawzah 'Ilmīyah* of Qum and joined the circle of students of 'Allāmah Ṭabāṭabā'ī. For the next seven years, the young Muhammad Ḥusayn studied in Qum receiving instruction from Shaykh Murtaḍā Hā'irī Yazdī, and Sayyid Muhammad Dāmād, in addition to 'Allāmah Ṭabāṭabā'ī. After seven years of studying with the 'Allāmah, Tihrānī reached the rank of *mujtahid* and decided to go to Najaf to continue his education. Tihrānī stayed in Najaf for seven years, during which time he studied with Āyatullāhs Āqā Buzurg Tihrānī, Sayyid Maḥmūd Shāhrūdī, Sayyid Abul-Qāsim Khu'ī, Shaykh Ḥusayn Ḥillī, and several other scholars.[4]

Several scholars and gnostics played important roles in 'Allāmah Tihrānī's spiritual life. As Tihrānī himself has stated, his first teacher and spiritual guide was 'Allāmah Ṭabāṭabā'ī, who initiated Tihrānī into gnosis *('irfān),* took him under his spiritual guidance, and closely supervised his wayfaring and spiritual advancement while he was studying in Qum. Until the end of his life, Tihrānī constantly admired Ṭabāṭabā'ī and acknowledged his role in his intellectual and spiritual achievements. Thus, when Tihrānī left Qum for Najaf, he had already started wayfaring and pursuing an active spiritual life.[5]

During the years in Najaf, as 'Allāmah Ṭabāṭabā'ī had instructed him, Tihrānī was to seek guidance in spiritual matters only from Āyatullāh 'Abbās Qūchānī and whomever he deemed appropriate. Āyatullāh Qūchānī taught Tihrānī further details and theoretical principles *(ẓawāhir)* of the doctrine. In 1376 A.H./1957 (solar 1336) Tihrānī met the most eminent spiritual master in Karbalā', namely, Ḥājj Sayyid Hāshim Ḥaddād (d. 1984), an incident that changed Tihrānī's soul and destiny.

'Allāmah Tihrānī states that he had heard Ḥājj Sayyid Hāshim Ḥaddād's name from 'Allāmah Ṭabāṭabā'ī who always spoke of him with respect and admiration. When he went to Najaf and visited Āyatullāh Shaykh 'Abbās Qūchānī, Tihrānī inquired about Ḥājj Sayyid Hāshim and found out that he lived in Karbalā'. A mysterious yearning to meet Sayyid

Hāshim finally led Tihrānī to make a pilgrimage to Karbalā'. In that same year he met the great master. The young Tihrānī's soul was totally captured by the spiritual eminence and charisma of Sayyid Hāshim Ḥaddād.[6]

Tihrānī's acquaintance with Sayyid Hāshim Ḥaddād had a profound impact on his scholarly and spiritual life. From his first meeting with Ḥaddād, the young Tihrānī's soul was greatly transformed. In Ḥaddād, Tihrānī found a sincere Muslim, and a great spiritual master and guide who had passed from the realm of multiplicity and was completely annihilated in Divine Unity *(tawḥīd):*

> . . . Sayyid Hāshim Ḥaddād was so absorbed in Divine Unity *(tawḥīd)* that words cannot describe his station and his personality. He was beyond description and comprehension. He was one of the most powerful figures in spiritual journeying who had passed beyond the realm of angels *(malakūt),* had reached the realm of Divine Names *(lāhūt)* and Divine Invincibility *(jabarūt)* and had been totally annihilated in the Divine Essence.[7]

One can hardly exaggerate the impact that Ḥaddād had on Tihrānī's spiritual life. In *Rūḥ-i mujarrad,* Tihrānī has described in detail Ḥaddād's spiritual station and the way he trained his disciples in spiritual matters. Suffice it to mention that after acquaintance with Ḥaddād until the master's death, Tihrānī made considerable advancement on the path, to such an extent that Ḥaddād honored Tihrānī by granting him the title of *"Sayyid al-Ṭāi'fatayn,"* Master of two peoples (i.e., scholars and gnostics).[8]

After seven years studying in Najaf and benefiting from Sayyid Hāshim Ḥaddād's presence and instructions, the master advised him to go back to Tehran. Despite his own desire, Tihrānī reluctantly returned to Iran and began his career as teacher, prayer leader, and orator in the Qā'im mosque in Tehran. In the meantime, by Ḥaddād's recommendation, Tihrānī took spiritual guidance from Shaykh Muhammad Jawād Anṣārī, another prominent master who lived in the city of Hamadān in western Iran.[9] For the next twenty-two years, Tihrānī visited Najaf and other shrine cities in Iraq regularly and greatly benefited from association with Ḥājj Sayyid Hāshim Ḥaddād. At the same time, he devoted most of his time and effort to preaching and spreading the principles of traditional Islām as well as teaching and training students who came to him from different parts of the country. In his public sermons, which were very popular, Tihrānī dealt with purely religious issues as well as sociopolitical questions. Some of these speeches were published later in Tehran or Mashhad.[9]

Sayyid Muhammad Ḥusayn Ḥusaynī was a traditional scholar in the true sense of the term, and highly respected in scholarly and religious circles in Tehran, Qum and Mashhad. Like his teacher and mentor, ʿAllāmah Ṭabāṭabāʾī, Tihrānī can be considered a student of the school of Muḥyī al-Dīn ibn al-ʿArabī, while at the same time being greatly influenced and inspired by the ideas and writings of Ṣadr al-Dīn Shīrāzī (Mullā Ṣadrā). He admired and respected Iranian philosophers of previous centuries, particularly such thinkers as Abū Rayḥān Bīrūnī, Ibn Sīnā, Naṣīr al-Dīn Ṭūsī, and Mullā Muḥsin Fayḍ Kāshānī. Frequently in his writings, Tihrānī referred to these thinkers and philosophers. In addition, he used verses from the Qurʾān extensively. Like ʿAllāmah Ṭabāṭabāʾī, he uses the same technique of commenting on and interpreting each verse with the help of other verses. As Thirānī states, this approach is based on certain *aḥādīth* of the Prophet and *rawāyāt* (narrations) of the Shīʿī Imāms, as well as on the *Nahj al-Balāghah* of Imām ʿAlī ibn Abī Ṭālib:

"إنَّ الْقُرْآنَ يُفَسِّرُ بَعْضُهُ بَعْضًا"

"Verily, some verses of the Qurʾān interpret and comment on some others."

and,

"كِتَابُ اللّهِ تُبْصِرُونَ بِهِ، وَتَنْطِقُونَ بِهِ وَتَسْمَعُونَ بِهِ، وَيَنْطِقُ بَعْضُهُ بِبَعْضٍ، يَشْهَدُ بَعْضُهُ عَلَى بَعْضٍ؛ لا يَخْتَلِفُ فِي اللّه، وَلا يُخَالِفُ بِصَاحِبِهِ عَنِ اللّهِ."

The Book of Allāh is the one by which you can see the Truth, say the Truth and hear the Truth. Some of its verses interpret other verses, some are witness and reason for others. The Qurʾān contains no contradictions in the affairs of Allāh and does not separate from Allāh whoever adheres to its injunctions.[10]

Another feature of Tihrānī's writings is his dealing with social, political, historical, moral, and philosophical issues, in addition to purely religious and metaphysical ones. In his writings, he addresses many questions facing contemporary Muslim society and provides appropriate Islamic solutions.[11]

Like 'Allāmah Ṭabāṭabā'ī, Āyatullāh Tihrānī devoted his life to scholarship as well as spiritual journeying and wayfaring. He wrote on metaphysics and a variety of Islamic subjects and expanded greatly our scope of understanding the relationship between Shī'ism and Sufism. His writings are characterized by their lucidity, originality and depth, and are indicative of his mastery of the Qur'ān, Shī'ism, Sufism, and Persian and Arabic literature. His spiritual orientation and his esoteric ideas were particularly influenced by teachings and instructions given to him by Hāshim Ḥaddād, as well as 'Allāmah Ṭabāṭabā'ī and Muhammad Jawād Anṣārī. Like them, he admired Muḥyī al-Dīn Ibn al-'Arabī, Shaykh Maḥmūd Shabastarī, Mawlānā Jalāl al-Dīn Rūmī, Ḥāfiẓ, and Ibn al-Fāriḍ. His devotion to these Sufi poets and thinkers is well reflected in his writings where he frequently presents relevant examples from their works. However, he was more outspoken than his teachers in criticizing the opponents of Sufism.

Āyatullāh Ḥusaynī Tihrānī was a teacher, eloquent speaker, and prolific writer. He wrote, edited, and translated numerous works on different aspects of Islām, Shī'ism, Sufism, eschatology and other related subjects. Like his teacher, Tihrānī's contributions to Islamic studies and gnosis earned him the honorable title of *'Allāmah* while he was still alive. Not only do these writings reflect the depth of his knowledge and mastery of philosophy, jurisprudence, theosophy, Shī'ism and the holy Qur'ān, they are also indicative of the purity of his heart, faith, sincerity and genuine yearning for knowledge and truth.

Another aspect of 'Allāmah Tihrānī's life that has not been examined to this day is his interest in politics and his participation in political activity during the two decades that preceded the Islamic Revolution of 1979. The nature and details of Tihrānī's political activities before, during, and after the Islamic Revolution are important issues that cannot be dealt with here and must be studied separately. The available information suggests that despite his preoccupation with preaching, teaching and writing, Tihrānī had turned his mosque into an active center of opposition against the Shāh's government before the revolution; and a center for mass mobilization and political education after the establishment of the Islamic Republic. In one of his publications, Tihrānī reports how he organized certain members of the clergy into small groups and defied the Shāh's government and its reforms in the early 1960s, how he urged Āyatullāh

Rūḥullāh Khomeinī to issue declarations against the government and formed networks for their distribution, and how he met or communicated with Āyatullāh Khomeinī and advised him on taking positions on different occasions. Of particular interest is Tihrānī's discussion of the events of 15 Khordad, 1342/June 5, 1963 and his activities in support of Khomeinī. When Khomeinī was arrested by government forces and the rumors of his upcoming execution spread, Tihrānī maintains that he met many prominent *'ulamā* of Qum and wrote to others in cities throughout Iran asking them to declare that Khomeinī was an Āyatullāh and one of the country's sources of emulation *(marja'-i taqlīd),* and therefore, his execution was not permissible according to the Constitution of 1905. As a result, instead of execution, Āyatullāh Khomeinī was sent to exile first to Turkey and then to Iraq. After the victory of the revolution, Tihrānī states, he met with Āyatullāh Khomeinī several times and presented the outline of a twenty-point program for consolidation of the new regime including the establishment of a new military force and suggestions to modify the new constitution.[12]

Despite his interest in politics, before the revolution Tihrānī concentrated most of his time and energy on an extensive cultural campaign for purification of Islām and Shī'ism from beliefs and practices he considered corrupt and non-Islamic. Concomitantly, he devoted himself to teaching, studying and practicing *'irfān* in a serious but quiet manner. We know that in the late 1960s and the 1970s, when 'Allāmah Ṭabāṭabā'ī conducted a class for a select group of his students in Tehran, the young Tihrānī, along with the late Āyatullāh Murtaḍā Muṭahharī and professors Henry Corbin and Seyyed Hossein Nasr, attended those sessions and benefited from 'Allāmah's knowledge and presence. During those sessions, important religious and intellectual questions on Islam in general, and Shī'ism and Sufism in particular, were discussed, and Professor Nasr acted as the main translator and interpreter.[13] After the Islamic Revolution of 1979 and the establishment of the Islamic Republic, Tihrānī settled in Mashhad where he devoted his time to teaching, writing and spiritual wayfaring. Many more students and aspirants of *'irfān* gathered around Tihrānī, benefited from his scholarship and received spiritual guidance from him until he passed away in 1416 A.H. /1995.[14]

As was mentioned before, 'Allāmah Tihrānī was initiated into the Divine mysteries while he was still fairly young. In Lubb al-Lubāb, 'Allāmah Ṭabāṭabā'ī discusses the doctrine and the method of the *ṭarīqah* (order) they both followed. In this order equal emphasis is placed on exoteric and esoteric aspects of Islām as well as on love and devotion to the Ahl al-Bayt of the Blessed Prophet (may peace and blessing be upon them). In *Lubb al-Lubāb,* Ṭabāṭabā'ī details these ideas and goes so far as to say that the station of the Universal Man *(al-insān al-kāmil)* can be fully attained only by the *Imām,* the status of the *Imām* in Shī'ism being identical to that of the Quṭb or Spiritual Pole in Sufism, whose existence in the world is always necessary and indispensable.

'Allāmah Tihrānī was a man of great piety and noble character. His presence is still felt strongly in the intellectual and spiritual circles in Mashhad several years after his departure from this world. Three years before his death in 1995 and with the support of his students and disciples, the 'Allāmah established in Mashhad the Foundation for Translation and Publication of the Collection on Islamic Sciences and Culture *(mu'assasa-yi tarjumah wa nashr-i dawra-yi 'ulūm wa ma'ārif-i islām).* He appointed some of his trusted students to manage and supervise the publication of his writings and the translation of some of those works into other languages. Most of the writings of the 'Allāmah had been published by Ḥikmat Publication Company while he was still alive. When he passed away, the Foundation took over this arduous task. To this date, the Foundation has published most of the writings of the 'Allāmah in Persian. Many of his works have also been translated into Arabic and published by *Dār al-muḥajjah al-bayḍā* in Beirut, Lebanon.[15] The *Lubb al-Lubāb* is the first in the series to be translated in its entirety into English. The comprehensive list of Tihrānī's publications will be presented in the coming pages. However, three of his publications, which he wrote on the *Nature of God, Imamology* and *Eschatology* are of particular interest and deserve special attention here.

Allāh Shināsī is a collection of speeches that the Āyatullāh gave in Mashhad. It starts with a commentary on the verses thirty-five through sixty-four of chapter twenty-four of the Qur'ān *(sūrat al-Nūr).* In this collection, he discusses some of the most profound metaphysical issues such as the Unity *(tawḥīd)* of the Divine Names, the Attributes, and the Essence; the descent of Divine Light in the manifestations of existence *(wujūd),* the reality of *walāyat,* the question of unity with the Divine, the meaning of *lā huwa illā huwa* (there is no he but He), and other related questions.

Imām Shināsī is an encyclopedic work in eighteen volumes based on the Qur'ān and the *Ḥadīth* that addresses the question of the *Imāmate* from historical, social, philosophical, and esoteric points of view, and the *imāmate* of Imām ʿAlī ibn Abī Ṭālib in particular. Important and often controversial issues such as the necessity for the presence of an infallible and living *Imām,* Prophetic traditions concerning the question of *walāyat,* the *Ghadīr-i Khumm* incident and the Farewell Pilgrimage of the Prophet *(ḥajjat al-widāʿ),* the development of Shīʿī sciences and the role of Imām Ṣādiq (may peace be upon him) and other issues of similar nature are discussed in this collection.

Maʿād Shināsī is another comprehensive work in ten volumes dealing with eschatology from the point of view of the Shīʿites. In this collection, ʿAllāmah Tihrānī deals with such questions as the intermediate world *(ʿālam-i barzakh),* the creation of Angels and their duties, life after death, and finally, resurrection and the day of judgment. Like his other works, this collection is also predominantly based on the Holy Qurʾān, *Ḥadīth,* and *rawāyāt* of the Shīʿite Imāms.

Other important books that Āyatullāh Ḥusayni Tihrānī wrote and have been published by the Foundation include the following:

1. *Hadīya-yi Ghadīrīyah* (The Ghadīrīyah Present)
2. *Lamaʿāt al-Ḥusayn* (Divine Flashes of [Imām] Ḥusayn)
3. *Lubb al-Lubāb dar sayr wa sulūk-i ulu'l-albāb* (Kernel of the Kernel Concerning the Wayfaring and Spiritual Journey of the People of Intellect)
4. *Mihr-i Tābān* (Shining Sun: A Biography of ʿAllāmah Ṭabāṭabāʾī)
5. *Nāmi-yi pīsh niwīs-i qānūn-i asāsī* (Introduction to the First Draft of the Constitution [of Iran])
6. *Nigarishī bar maqāla-yi basṭ wa qabḍ-i turīk-i sharīʿat bih qalam-i ductur ʿAbd al-Karīm Surūsh* (An Examination of the Essay by Dr. ʿAbdulkarim Surush on the Theoretical Expansion and Contraction in the Sharīʿah)
7. *Nūr-i malakūt-i Qurʾān* (The Angelic Light of the Qurʾān) [in 4 volumes]
8. *Risāla-yi badīʿah* (The Original Treatise) [in Arabic]
9. *Risālah ḥawl-i masʾala-yi ruʾyat-i hilāl* (Treatise on Seeing the Moon)
10. *Risāla-yi nikāḥīyah* (Treatise on Marriage)
11. *Risāla-yi nuwīn* (The New Treatise)
12. *Risāla-yi sayr wa sulūk* (Treatise on Wayfaring and Spiritual Journey Attributed to Sayyid Mahdī Baḥr al-ʿUlūm) [edited with an introduction and comments]

13. *Rūḥ-i Mujarrad* (The Detached Soul)
14. *Tawḥīd-i ʿilmī wa ʿaynī* (Objective and Intellectual Tawḥīd)
15. *Walāyat-i faqīh dar ḥukūmat-i islām* (The Rule of Juristconsult in the Islamic Government)
16. *Waẓīfa-yi fard-i musalmān dar iḥyāʾ-i ḥukūmat-i islām* (The Duty of Individual Muslims in Reviving Islamic Government)

Sections of *Lubb al-Lubāb,* as well as selected parts of *Rūḥ-i Mujarrad,* were previously rendered into English by Mr. ʿAlī Qulī Qarāʾī and appeared in *Tawḥīd,* a quarterly journal that was once published in the city of Qum, though its publication has ceased for some time. I consulted Mr. Qarāʾī's translation from time to time. I would like to express my sincere appreciation to him for sharing his wisdom with me. The present translation is the first scholarly and complete translation of *Lubb al-Lubāb* with explanatory notes for specialist and non-specialist readers alike.

The present translation owes its completion to several scholars and friends. To Professor Seyyed Hossein Nasr I am eternally indebted for his friendship and guidance that spans over many years. I am especially grateful to him for suggesting this book for translation and generously providing perceptive comments and advice and kindly writing a preface, despite his extremely busy schedule. Special thanks are due to three anonymous scholars who evaluated the manuscript for the State University of New York Press and recommended its publication. I am indebted to them for their perceptive comments and suggestions, which greatly improved the quality of the final translation. I would like also to thank several friends, including Arin McNamara, Joseph Lumbard, David Dakake, and Lawrence Meehan, who read an earlier version of the manuscript and provided excellent editorial comments and suggestions; and to Ms. Nancy Ellegate and Mrs. Dana Foote of SUNY Press for their patience, support and hard work in the process of publication of this book. I am very grateful to the Foundation for Translation and Publication of the Collection on Islamic Sciences and Civilization *(muʾassasa-yi tarjumah wa nashr-i dawrah-i ʿulūm wa maʿārif-i islām)* in Mashhad, Iran, for granting permission to me to translate this book into English.

Last but not least, I am particularly indebted to my children Parand and Amīrpooyān, and to my wife Sarah for creating an island of stability at home, enabling and always encouraging me to pursue my scholarly work despite her own professional commitments and other responsibilities. Words cannot describe my appreciation of her angelic qualities of purity, sincerity, dedication, and patience throughout the last thirty-two years of our life together, and in the process of preparation of this work. It is to her, to my mother, and to the memory of my father who was a pure-hearted wayfarer in the path of *'irfān* for over seventy years that this work is dedicated.

In the process of preparing this manuscript, it was proved time and again that the saving grace of the *wilāyat* of the Ahl al-Bayt of the Blessed Prophet has no limits and knows no boundaries or distance. Ever since I started this project, I have been showered with special blessings from the sacred grace and *barakah* of Imām 'Alī ibn Mūsā al-Riḍā, may peace be upon him, despite being some ten thousand miles away from his sacred precinct in Mashhad.[16]

In translating technical terms and phrases I have benefited greatly from previous works on Sufism, particularly books by R. A. Nicholson, A. J. Arberry, T. Izutsu, A. M. Schimmel, F. Schuon, T. Burckhardt, Seyyed Hossein Nasr, Martin Lings, Mehdi Hā'iri, William Chittick, Sachiko Murata, and many other scholars. I have also supplied explanatory notes and references for technical terms taken from the Qur'ān and *ḥadīth*. Qur'ānic verses have been translated in consultation with the translation of the Holy Book by Marmaduke Pickthall. For *Aḥādīth* and *rawāyāt,* I have supplied translation after consultation and exchange of ideas with other colleagues and friends. Needless to say, none of the above individuals are responsible for any errors or shortcomings in the translation of the text and technical terms. The responsibility for any such mistakes is solely my own. It is sincerely hoped that this humble contribution will open new doors and help our readers to understand the relationship between Islām, Shī'ism and Sufism, particularly at a time when both are greatly misrepresented by pseudo-Sufis and pseudo-Shī'ites and misunderstood by so many lay readers in the Muslim world and in the West. *bi mannihī wa karamihī.*

Notes

1. For a brief description of Āyatullāh Muhammad Ṣādiq Tihrānī's activities against Riḍā Shāh's government, see 'Allāmah Tihrānī, *Waẓīfa-yi*

fard-i musalmān dar iḥyā-'yi ḥukūmat-i islām, compiled and edited by Muḥsin Saī'īdiān (Tihran), 1410 A.H. /1989. For an account of the 'ulamā's reaction to Riḍā Shah's government and his policies, see Mohammad H. Faghfoory, "Ulama-State Relations in Iran: 1921–1941," in *International Journal of Middle East Studies,* 19 (November 1987):413–432; and "The Impact of Modernization on the Ulama in Iran: 1925–1941," in *Journal of Iranian Studies,* 26:3–4 (Summer–Fall 1993):277–312.

2. For a short biography of 'Allāmah Ṭabāṭabā'ī in English, see Seyyed Hossein Nasr's introduction to Ṭabāṭabā'ī's *Shī'ite Islām,* translated from the Persian (Albany: State University of New York Press), 1975. For his biography in Persian, see 'Allāmah Muhammad Ḥusayn Ḥusayni Tihrānī, *Mihr-i Tābān* (Mashhad, Iran: University of Mashhad Press), A.H. 1417/1996.
3. *Mu'assasa-yi Tarjumah wa Nashr,* "Notes on the Life and Career of 'Allāmah Tihrānī."
4. Ibid.
5. See *Mihr-i Tābān,* pp. 23 and 45–48.
6. For a comprehensive biography of Ḥājj Sayyid Hāshim Ḥaddād and his role in the 'Allāmah's spiritual life, see *Rūḥ-i Mujarrad* (Tehran: Intishārāt-i Ḥikmat), 1414 A.H. /1995. This book contains useful information on important contemporary *'ulamā* of Qum and Najaf, including Āyatullāhs Ḥājj Mīrzā 'Alī Āqā Qāḍī, Muhammad Jawād Anṣārī, and many others with whom the 'Allāmah had studied or associated.
7. *Rūḥ-i Mujarrad,* pp. 22. See also *Mu'assasa-yi Tarjumah wa Nashr,* op. cit.
8. *Rūḥ-i Mujarrad,* p. 23, and 33–37. Also see Mu'assasa-yi Tarjumah wa Nashr.
9. See, for example, *Nūr-i malakūt-i Qur'ān* (Tehran, 1410–1417 A.H. / 1990–1996; *Risāla-yi badī'ah* (Mashhad, 1418 A.H. /1997), *Kāhish-i Jam'īyat: Ḍarba-yi sahmgīn bar Paykar-i Muslimīn* (Tehran, 1415 A.H. /1994), and *Nigarishī bar maqāla-yi basṭ wa qabḍ-i turīk-i sharī'at bih qalam-i ductur 'Abd al-Karīm Surūsh* (Tehran, 1415 A.H. /1994).
10. Imām 'Alī ibn Abī Ṭālib, *Nahj al-Balāghah,* discourse #133, p. 414 (Tehran, 1351, Lunar/1972).
11. See, in particular, *Nūr-i malakūt-i Qur'ān, Risāla-yi badī'ah, Nigarishī bar maqālah . . . , Waẕīfa-yi fard-i musalmān.* op. cit.

13. See *Mihr-i Tābān*, pp. 61–78; and Nasr, "Introduction," op. cit. p. 24.
14. *Mu'assasa-yi Tarjumah wa Nashr*, op. cit.
15. Ibid.
16. Of all the Shī'ī Imāms, only the shrine of the eighth Imām, 'Alī ibn Mūsā al-Riḍā, is located in Iran in the city of Mashhad. The holy shrine of the first Shī'ī Imām, 'Alī ibn Abī Ṭālib, is in Najaf, and that of the third Imām, Ḥusayn ibn 'Alī, is located in the city of Karbalā' in Iraq.

I

Editor's Introduction

The Straight Path Is One Which Combines the Exoteric and the Esoteric

In the Name of Allāh, the Beneficent, the Merciful

May Allāh's most exalted blessings be upon the immaculate spirit of the Seal of prophets, Muhammad al-Muṣṭafā, and his noble deputy and spiritual heir *(waṣī)* and possessor of the greatest sanctity *(wilāyah),* 'Alī al-Murtaḍā, and his glorious descendants, the Pure Imāms—especially the Pole of the contingent realm, the *baqiyyat 'allāh,* and His Proof *(ḥujjah),* son of al-Ḥasan al-'Askarī—may our souls be sacrificed for him.

The love of religion, the attraction toward the realm of the Invisible *(ghayb),* and the yearning to discover the mysteries of the world beyond matter are part of man's instinct and inherent in his nature. This yearning emanates from the power of Divine Attraction of the Lord that pulls the contingent world, especially the noblest of human beings, toward His boundless and Infinite station. The magnet that draws the soul is that very Soul of souls, which is interpreted in various terms as the Beloved *(jānān),* the Reality of all realities *(ḥaqīqat al-haqā'iq),* the Eternal Principle *(aṣl-i qadīm),* the Source of Beauty *(manba'-i jamāl),* the Beginning of Being *(mabda' al-wujūd),* and the Ultimate of Perfection *(ghāyat al-kamāl).*

الكُلُّ عِبَارَةٌ وَأَنْتَ المَعْنَى   يَا مَنْ هُوَ لِلْقُلُوبِ مَغْنَاطِيسٌ

The universe is expression and Thou art its meaning,
O, Thou! Who art the magnet of the hearts.[1]

This magnetic attraction to the Truth, which results in tearing apart natural boundaries and limitations of the soul and traversing toward the realm of catharsis and boundlessness and, ultimately, annihilation in the Act, Names, Attributes, and Sacred Essence of [Allāh who is] the Origin of all origins, the Ultimate Goal of all goals, and the Worshiped One in whose Subsistence all being subsists; is more exalted and more magnificent than any act that can come to imagination.

جَذْبَةٌ مِنْ جَذَبَاتِ الرَّحْمَنِ تُوَازِي عِبَادَةَ الثَّقَلَيْنِ

> A single attraction from God, the Most Compassionate, outbalances the worship of all men and *jinn.*

In the center of his innate nature and essence, man finds a desire to move toward this cynosure of all quests and the pivot *(qiblah)* of worship. With the God-given power of instinct and primordial nature, man sets out on a journey and with all his being goes toward that direction. Therefore, in the course of the journey all his bodily organs and his total being must be put to work to perform their functions. The physical world and corporeal faculties, which constitute his physical nature *(ṭabʿ),* the imaginal and archetypal world that constitute his intermediate world *(barzakh),* and the realm of intellect and spirit that constitute his reality, all must participate in this journey and collaborate with each other.

The body should turn toward the *Kaʿbah,* and set itself to stand [before God], bowing and prostrating, and performing the daily prayer *(ṣalāt),* the mind must keep itself immune from distracting memories and turn to [and concentrate on] the Lote Tree *(sidrat al-muntahā).*[2] The soul must be immersed in the light of the abode of Divine Sanctuary, and become intoxicated and annihilated in the Sacred Precinct of the One.

It becomes clear from the above discussion how cut off from the Real Goal and how far away from witnessing His Beauty are those people who preoccupy themselves solely with the outward, are satisfied with the crust rather than with the kernel and the essence, and from among all prayers and good deeds confine themselves to bodily movements. By the same token, those who are solely in search of inner meaning and evade observing the blessed rituals and rites of worship as prescribed by the *Sharīʿah,* are far from the reality. They [are the ones who] have been content with derivatives and metaphors *(majāz)* instead of the truth, and with imagination and illusion rather than reality.

Is it not true that the light of God is immanent in all His manifestations in the realm of contingency? If so, why should we exclude the body from worship, close this microcosm to the theophany of Divine Light, and preoccupy ourselves and be content with such terms as "union" *(wuṣūl),* "kernel" *(lubb),* "essence" *(dhāt),* and "inward prayer"? Would that not be a one-dimensional and one-sided worship?

As to the middle position *(al-namaṭ al-awsaṭ)* and the median community *(ummatan wasaṭan)*[3] they are those groups of people who have combined the outward *(ẓāhir)* and the inward *(bāṭin)* within themselves, have made all levels and planes of their being worship the Beloved and submit to Him, and have prepared themselves adequately for this heavenly journey. They have made the outward a reflection of the inward, and the inward the soul and the reality of the outward, and have blended the two together as milk and sugar. They consider the outward as a means to reach the inward and regard the inward devoid of the outward as scattered motes *(haba'an manthūrā).*[4] (Holy Qur'ān, 25:23).

اَللّٰهُمَّ نَوِّرْ ظَاهِرِي بِطَاعَتِكَ، وَبَاطِنِي بِمَحَبَّتِكَ، وَقَلْبِي بِمَعْرِفَتِكَ، وَرُوحِي بِمُشَاهَدَتِكَ، وَسِرِّي بِاسْتِقْلَالِ اتِّصَالِ حَضْرَتِكَ، يَا ذَا لْجَلَالِ وَالإِكْرَامِ.

O God, illuminate my outward with [the light of] obedience to Thee and my inner being with Thy Love, my heart with knowledge of Thee, my spirit with Thy vision, and my inmost consciousness *(sirr)* with the independence of attachment to Thy Threshold, O Lord of Majesty and Munificence.[5]

The above discussion makes it abundantly clear that in order to guide the soul toward spiritual perfection and traverse through the phases and stages of human perfection, reliance on acquiring intellectual and contemplative sacred sciences, such as teaching and/or learning philosophy, will not be sufficient at all. Although syllogism *(qiyās)* and rational reasoning *(burhān)* based on valid premises and sound logic can offer the mind convincing conclusions, nonetheless, they do not satisfy the heart and the soul, and cannot quench the spirit's thirst for attaining the truths and witnessing the intuitive subtleties.

It is true that the sciences of theosophy and philosophy are genuine and indubitable sciences, constitute the noblest of all intellectual and contemplative sciences, and have established the idea of the Divine Unity *(tawḥīd)* on the basis of reason and have closed the door to any kind of doubt or uncertainty. It is also true that the Glorious Qur'ān as well as many traditions of the Immaculate Shī'ite Imāms—who are guardians and protectors of Revelation and prophethood, and steadfast in knowledge and religion *(rāsikhūn fi'l 'ilm)*—emphasized and prescribed contemplation, intellection, logic, reason, and rational argumentation.[6] However, it is a futile attempt to rely solely on the rational and philosophical [approach to] *tawḥīd,* as followers of the rationalist school do, without submission of the heart, the inmost consciousness *(wijdān-i ḍamīr),* and to inward witnessing *(shuhūd-i bāṭin).*

To deprive the heart and the inward of spiritual nourishment emanating from the Invisible World, and of Divine rays of Heavenly Beauty and Majesty, and to content oneself to cruise through books, libraries, schools, and courses of study or teaching even at the highest level amounts to satisfying the needs of only one faculty and leaving higher faculties unnurtured. The Distinguished Religion, which is based on the straight path, observes both aspects, brings perfection to all faculties, and actualizes the hidden potentials and capabilities of the human being in both directions. On the one hand, it encourages intellection and contemplation, and on the other hand, commands one to cleanse and purify the heart from contamination of carnal desires, so that one can find peace, serenity, and tranquillity in one's heart. As the Holy Qur'ān declares after reciting eleven majestic oaths:

قد أفْلَحَ مَنْ زَكَّيهَا وَقَدْ خَابَ مَنْ دَسَّيهَا

Whoever purifies it finds deliverance,
whoever corrupts it loses. (91:9–10)

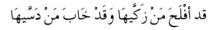

These Qur'ānic verses, which address the human soul and speak to man's inner self, summon individuals from among thinkers, scholars, teachers of philosophy, and masters of intellectual reasoning to servitude *(ta'abbud)*, attentive regard *(murāqabah)*, and accounting of one's inward state *(muḥāsabah);* so that, by sincere acts exclusively for God's pleasure, the springs of Divine Knowledge may spout forth from the depth of their hearts and flow out to their tongues; and eventually the thundering flow of thoughts, inspirations, and Merciful Divine intuition will gush forth from the center of their being, as the Prophet stated:

مَنْ أَخْلَصَ لِلَّه أَرْبَعِينَ صَبَاحاً ظَهَرَتْ يَنَابِيعُ الْحِكْمَةِ مِنْ قَلْبِهِ إِلَى

لِسَانِهِ.

Whoever sincerely purifies his heart for God for forty days will find springs of wisdom gush forth from his heart and flow toward his tongue.[7]

Ṣadr al-Mut'allihīn Shīrāzī, the pride of the philosophers of the East, or rather of the world, spent a lifetime on [studying and teaching] transcendental theosophy *(al-ḥikmat al-muta'ālīyah)*, but finally was so immersed in the worship of God and servitude to Him and in purification of the inmost consciousness that he wrote eloquently in the introduction to his *Asfār-i arba'ah:*

وَإِنِّي لأَسْتَغْفِرُ اللّه كَثِيرَ مِمَّا ضَيَّعْتُ شَطْراً مِن عُمْرِي في تَتَبُّعِ آرَاءِ

المُتَفَلْسِفَةِ المُجَادِلِينَ مِنْ أَهْلِ الكَلامِ وَتَدَ قَبقاتِهِم وَتَعَلُّمِ جُرْبُزَتِهِم في

القَوْلِ وتَفَنُّنِهِم في البَحْثِ حتَّى تَبَيَّنَ لِي آخِرَ الأَمْرِ بِنُورِ الإِيمَانِ وتأيِيد

اللّه المَنّانِ إِنّ قِياسَهُمْ عَقِيم وصِراطَهُم غَيْر مُسْتَقِيمٍ؛ فأَلْقَينا زَمَامَ أَمْرِنا

إِلَيْه وإِلى رَسُولِهِ النَّذِير المُنْذِرِ، فَكُلّ ما بَلَغَنَا مِنْهُ آمَنَّا بِه وصَدَّقْناهُ ولَمْ

نحتَلْ أَن نُخَبِّل لهُ وَجْهاً عَقْلِيّاً ومَسْلَكاً بَحْثِيّاً بلْ اقْتَدَيْنَا بِهُدَاهُ وانْتَهَيْنَا

بِنَهْيِهِ إِمْتِثَالًا لِقَوْلِهِ تَعَالَى : «(مَا أَتَاكُمُ الرَّسُولُ فَخُذُوهُ وَمَا نَهَاكُمْ عَنْهُ

فَانْتَهوا)»، حَتَّى فَتَحَ اللّهُ عَلَى قَلْبِنَا مَا فَتَحَ فَأَفْلَحَ بِبَرَكَةِ مُتَابَعَته وأَنْجَحَ.

Indeed, I seek profuse forgiveness from God for having wasted a part of my life studying the opinions of the pseudo-philosophers and the polemicists from among the theologians and the intricacies of their discussions, learning their clever tactics of speech and their arts of debate, until at last with the light of faith and the assistance of God, the Munificent, it became clear to me that their syllogisms were sterile and their path not straight. Thereafter, I surrendered my affair to Him and His Messenger, the Warner and the Warned, believed earnestly in all that had reached us from him, accepting it without making any attempt to find some rational justification or scholarly interpretation for it. Rather, I followed His Prophet's guidance, refrained from what was forbidden, and submitted to his injunction—as God, the Exalted has said: "Take and follow whatever injunctions the Messenger brings you and refrain from what he forbids you" (Qur'ān, 59:7)—until God opened my heart to what He willed, and by the grace of following His Prophet, I was delivered and saved. (*al-Asfār al-arbaʿah,* Introduction)[8]

It is appropriate here to remember the most celebrated, the eternal jurist, Lordly sage, and Divinely inspired gnostic who lived at the beginning of the last century, namely, the Sign of the Truth *(āyat al-Ḥaqq)* Ākhūnd Mawlā Ḥusayn Qulī Hamadānī. This great jurist, unrivaled thinker, and exalted philosopher incorporated all true sciences in light of the science of gnosis and purification of the soul; and combined all of them in the lights of the Divine Image, assigned to every science its appropriate place and status, and considered attainment to the Divine Sanctuary as the ultimate goal. He trained many students and presented them to the world of gnosis. Each one of them became a shining star in the firmament of virtues and *tawḥīd,* and illuminated the world with the rays of his insight and wisdom. Among them one can mention Āqā Sayyid Aḥmad Karbalā'ī who was a saintly gnostic, and his student Ḥājj Mīrzā ʿAlī Āqā

Qāḍī, the pride of the jurists and the pearl of the gnostics, may God elevate their noble stations.

The pride of all commentators and the guide of seekers of the Truth, our revered teacher, His Holiness Āyatullāh 'Allāmah Sayyid Muḥammad Ḥusayn Ṭabāṭabā'ī, may God prolong his ennobling presence, had from the first days of life been flying on the two wings of knowledge and action, and had traveled on the path of philosophy as well as gnosis under the tutelage of the late Āyatullāh Qāḍī. He spent his entire life mastering syllogism, reason and oratory, and devoted himself to advancing the intellectual sciences and activities [e.g., working on] the *Ishārāt [Ishārāt wa Tanbihāt],* and the *Shifā'* [of Ibn Sīnā] and the *Asfār* [*Asfār-i arba'ah* of Mullā Ṣadrā], and writing commentaries on them. At the same time he was totally preoccupied with inward retreat and Divine mysteries and constant attention *(murāqabah),* until finally he landed at the sacred threshold of the Qur'ān. He became so immersed in the praiseworthy verses of the Qur'ān that recitation and interpretation of those verses, contemplation, and symbolic interpretation *(ta'wīl)* and commenting upon them became a more important preoccupation for him than any other contemplative activity. For him contemplation on the verses of the Qur'ān was a more exalted and more pleasing activity than any discursive reasoning as though he had given up everything but total submission and servitude to the Master of the majestic *Sharī'ah* and his honored deputies and spiritual heirs *(awṣiyā').*

Our honored friend and eminent master, kinder than any brother, the late Āyatullāh Shaykh Murtaḍā Muṭahharī[9] with whom my friendship extended over thirty-five years, may God bestow His pleasure upon him, had a brilliant mind and critical vision. He spent a lifetime studying, teaching, writing, preaching, and investigating and seeking the truth on issues related to philosophy. However, thanks to his alert mind and critical soul, in the last few years of his life he fully realized that one cannot find inner peace without reaching the inward and without connecting with the Munificent Lord. He learned that without quenching one's thirsty heart at the wellspring of Divine effusion, one cannot attain serenity and inner peace and will never be able to enter the sacred sanctuary of God, or circumambulate around it and reach the *Ka'bah* that one yearns for. So Muṭahharī entered the path like a candle that burns constantly and dissolves, or like a moth that flings itself into the fire. Like a passionate and committed believer overwhelmed by fervor and annihilated in the shoreless ocean of the Names, Attributes, and the Essence of the Worshiped One, and whose whole being grew infinitely drawing on the infinitude of the Divine Being, Muṭahharī stepped into the center of this vast arena. His wayfaring was characterized by frequent night vigils, lamentation, and invocation in the solitude of the dawn, immersion in contemplation and invocation, persistent devotion to learning lessons of the Qur'ān, withdrawal from world-loving people and slaves of desire, and association with God-fearing people and friends *(awliyā')* of God. May God's endless mercy be upon him:

لِمثِْل هَذا فَلْيَعْمَل العَامِلُون

And for the like of this let the workers toil! (Qur'ān, 37:61)

إنَّ اللّه مَعَ الّذين أتّقوا و الَّذِينَ هُم مُحْسِنُون

Indeed God is with those who keep their duty unto Him and those who are doers of good. (Qur'ān, 16:128)

Some time ago they asked this humble being to write something on the occasion of the commemoration of Āyatullāh Muṭahharī's martyrdom. Poor being that I am, I considered myself unqualified for the task and refused to accept such an assignment due also to my preoccupation with and involvement in other responsibilities. More recently, when that request was brought up again the spirit of that honored friend came to my assistance; therefore, I wrote down these short passages and attached them as an introduction to a treatise that I had compiled on wayfaring and spiritual journey, and made it available, for the pleasure of the exalted soul of my departed friend, to the seekers of the Truth and the wayfarers on the path of Truth and Peace.

بِيَدِهِ أزِمَّةُ الأُمُورِ وَبِهِ أسْتَعِينُ.

In His hands are the reins of all affairs and it is His help that I seek.

As to its origin, the seeds of this treatise in essence were the first round of lessons on ethics and gnosis delivered to a selected group of students in the theological school *(Ḥawza-yi ʿilmīyah)* in Qum in A.H. 1368/1949–1369/1950 by our revered master and teacher, Āyatullāh ʿAllāmah Muḥammad Ḥusayn Ṭabāṭabāʾī, may my soul be ransomed for him. This humble being had taken notes during those sessions and often referred to them. I always found them a source of spiritual illumination and comfort for my soul during times of distress, contraction, and tedium. The present book is, indeed, the revised and greatly expanded version of those class notes with some elaboration and additions. Whatever spiritual rewards there may be in this undertaking is dedicated to the spirit of that honorable friend, the late Āyatullāh Murtaḍā Muṭahharī, may God elevate his noble station.

اللَّهُمَّ احْشُرْهُ مَعَ أَوْلِيَائِكَ الْمُقَرَّبِينَ، وَاخْلُفْ عَلى عَقِبِهِ فِي الْغَابِرِينَ،

وَاجْعَلْهُ مِنْ رُفَقَاءِ مُحَمَّدٍ وَآلِهِ الطَّاهِرِينَ، وَارْحَمْهُ وَإِيَّانَا بِرَحْمَتِكَ يَا

أَرْحَمَ الرَّاحِمِينَ، بيده أزمة الأمور وبه نستعين.

> O God, gather him with Your intimate friends *(awliyāʾ)* and be protector of his descendants in the future, and place him among the companions of Muhammad and his immaculate Household, and be merciful to him, and to us, for the sake of Your Mercy, O Most Merciful of the merciful.

Notes

1. Sabzawārī, Mullā Muhammad Hādī, *Manẓūma-yi Ilāhīyāt fi afʿālihī taʿālā ghurar fi anḥāʾ taqsīmāt li fiʿl Allāh Taʿālā,* Nāṣiri ed., p. 183.
2. *Sidrat al muntahā* is considered the highest grade of existence of the outermost region of the cosmos. Higher than that is the immediate proximity to God described as *qāb al-qawsayn* or the distance of two bows where the Prophet was taken on the night of his ascension to

Heaven, or *laylat al-mi'rāj*. See Seyyed Hossein Nasr, *Muhammad: Man of God* (London: Muhammadi Trust, 1982) p. 14. See also Martin Lings, *Muhammad: His Life Based on the Earliest Sources* 2nd ed. (Cambridge: Islamic Text Society, 1991), (Rochester, Vermont: Inner Traditions International, 1983), pp. 102–103.

3. On several occasions the holy Qur'ān calls Muslims the median community. See for instance 2: 143.

   We have appointed you a middle nation that you may be witness against mankind, and the messenger may be a witness against you.

   وَكَذَلِكَ جَعَلْنَاكُم أمةً وَسَطًا لِتَكُونُوا شُهَدَاءَ عَلَى النَاسِ ويَكُونَ الرَسُولُ عَلَيْكُم شَهِيداً.

4. *And We shall turn what act they commited and make it scattered motes.* Holy Qur'ān, 25:23
5. This prayer is cited from a supplication attributed to Amīr al-Mu'minīn 'Imām 'Alī, may peace be upon him, expounded by Ḥājj Mawlā Kabūtar-Āhangī and has been published in a pocket-size edition. In his book, *Kalamāt-i maknūnah,* Mullā Muḥsin Fayḍ Kāshānī says that this prayer has been mentioned in the supplications of the Imāms, may peace be upon them. For a short biography of Kabūtar-Āhangī, see Mas'ūod Homāyūnī, *Tārīkh-i silsilahhā-yi ṭarīqah-yi ni'matullāhīyah dar irān* (Tehran, 1358–1979), pp. 92–94.
6. Holy Qur'ān, 3:7, and 4:162.
7. This sacred tradition has been narrated from the Messenger of God through several chains of authority with different wordings but with the same meaning. It is cited in *Iḥya' 'ulūm al-Dīn* [of Imāmā Muhammad Ghazzālī], vol. 4, pp. 322; and its glossary on p. 191. It is also cited in *'Awārif al-ma'ārif* published on the margins of *Iḥyā al-'ulūm,* ii, 265. Among other Shī'ī sources, it is cited in *'Uy'ūn akhbār al-riḍā* (by 'Alī ibn Mūsā al-riḍā, the eighth Imām), p. 258, *'Uddat al-dā'ī,* p. 170, and *Uṣūl al-Kāfī* (Muhammad ibn Ya'qub al-Kulaynī), vol. II, pp. 16. The tradition is cited in the *'Uyūn al-Akhbār,* along with the chain of authorities from *ḥaḍrat Imām al-Riḍā,* may peace be upon him, from his father, from his grandfather, from *ḥaḍrat* Muhammad ibn 'Alī al-Bāqir, from his father, *ḥaḍrat* Sajjād, from

Jābir ibn 'Abd Allāh al-Anṣārī, and finally from Amīr al-Mu'minīn, may peace be upon him.

In his book entitled *Rūḥ-i Mujarrad,* Āyatullāh Sayyid Muhammad Ḥusayni Tihrānī quotes the following explanation from his spiritual master, Sayyid Hāshim Ḥaddād, concerning different kinds of thoughts: "Thoughts are of four categories. First, those which are sacred and these are thoughts that turn one's attention away from oneself and toward God and call one to Him. Second, satanic thoughts that make one oblivious to God, and cause anger, enmity, greed, and envy to grow in one's heart. Third, the Heavenly *(malakūtī)* thoughts are those that lead human beings toward the worship of God and fear of Him. Fourth, the psychic *(nafsānī)* thoughts which allure one toward the world's adornments and desires. Human beings have a sublime faculty which can turn all satanic and psychic thoughts into virtues, and employ all of them in the way of God so that the earning of wealth, fulfillment of desires, and the cultivation of adornments all are done for the sake of God, and not for the self. He also has a faculty that is higher and can transform all those thoughts, including spiritual thoughts, into Divine thoughts; leading one to regard them as ensuing from God, and encountering nothing save God."

8. Ṣadr al-Dīn Shīrāzī, known as Mullā Ṣadrā (979–1050/1571–1640).
9. Āyatullāh Shaykh Murtaḍā Muṭahharī (d. 1358/1979) an Islamic scholar and activist who studied with 'Allāmah Ṭabāṭabā'ī in Qum and received modern education at the University of Tehran. He was a major intellectual force and theoretician of the Islamic revolution who was assassinated in 1979. Among his writings are, *Nahḍathā-yi Eslāmī dar Ṣad Sāl-i Akhīr* (Tehran, 1978); *Pīrāmmon-i Enqilāb-i Eslāmī* (Tehran, 1892), *Islām wa muqtaḍīyāt-i zamān* (Tehran, 1983), and numerous other works.

2

He Is the Almighty

Risāla-yi Lubb al-Lubāb dar Sayr wa Sulūk-i Ulu'l Albāb
Treatise on the Kernel of the Kernel
Concerning the Wayfaring and Spiritual Journey
of the People of Intellect

بِسْمِ اللّٰهِ الرَّحْمَانِ الرَّحِيم

وَصَلَّى اللّٰهُ عَلَى مُحَمَّدٍ وَآلِهِ الطَّاهِرِينَ، وَلَعْنَةُ اللّٰهِ عَلَى أعْدَائِهِمْ

أجْمَعِينَ. وَبَعْدُ قَالَ اللّٰه العَلِيُّ العَظِيمُ:

In the Name of Allāh, the Most Beneficent, the Most Merciful.
May God's greeting be upon Muhammad and his immaculate Household and may God's curse be upon all their enemies.

سَنُرِيهِمْ آيَاتِنَا فِي الآفَاقِ وَفِي أنْفُسِهِمْ حَتَّى يَتَبَيَّنَ لَهُمْ أنَّهُ الحَقُّ أو لَمْ

يَكْفِ بِرَبِّكَ أنَّهُ عَلَى كُلِّ شَيءٍ شَهِيد ألاَ أنَّهُمْ فِي مِرْيَةٍ مِنْ لِقَاءِ رَبِّهِمْ

ألا أنَّهُ بِكُلِّ شَيءٍ مُحِيطٌ.

God, Exalted and Almighty, has said:

> We shall show them Our signs on the horizons and within themselves, until it will become clear to them that He is the Truth. Doth not thy Lord suffice, since He is Witness over all things? Behold! Are they still in doubt about the meeting with their Lord? Lo! Is not He surrounding all things? (Qur'ān, 41:53–54)

چه مبارك سحری بود و چه فرخنده شبی

آن شب قدر که این تازه براتم دادند

بی خود از شعشعهٔ پرتو ذاتم کردند

باده از جام تجلّیِ صفاتم دادند

What a blessed dawn! What an auspicious night!
Night of Power, when they granted me this New Transference,
By the rays of the lights of His Essence, they made me selfless
And offered me the wine of theophany of His Attributes. (Ḥāfiẓ)

The profane human being lives in the dark wilderness of materialism, and dwells helplessly in the midst of the shoreless ocean of lusts and multiplicities. Every moment he is tossed by the waves of material attachments. Before he can recover from the injuries of one stroke and pull himself together, he is knocked down by another, a more frightening and terrorizing wave that arises from his attachment to possessions and wealth, and wife and children. The waves of these attachments constantly slap him in the face and draw him into the depth of the dark and terrifying ocean to the extent that his wailing and appeal fade away in the uproar of the waves. Regardless of which direction he turns, he realizes that anguish and remorse, which are indispensable characteristics of perishable matter, frighten and threaten him. In the midst of all this, occasionally he is caressed by the life-giving and refreshing breeze of Divine Attraction *(jadhbah).* He feels that this loving breeze pulls him in a direction and toward an unknown destination. However, the breeze of Divine Attraction is not permanent and only blows every once in a while.

وَإِنَّ لِرَبِّكُمْ فِي آيَامِ دَهْرِكُمْ نَفَحَاتٍ أَلاَ فَتَعَرَّضُوا لَهَا وَلاَ تُعْرِضُوا عَنْهَا.

Verily, in the days of your life there will come to you wafts of Divine breaths from your Lord. Be aware [when they blow]; turn to them and do not turn [your face] away from them.

During such moments the traveler on the path of God feels new blood in his veins, and under the effect of that very Divine attraction, decides to go beyond the realms of multiplicity, and by all possible means, prepares provisions and starts a journey to free himself of this tormented and perilous tumult. In the terminology of the gnostics *('urafā)* this journey is called wayfaring and spiritual journeying *(sayr wa sulūk). Sulūk* means traveling along the path, while *sayr* means observing particularities and marvels of stages and phases encountered on the way. The provisions *(zād)* required for this spiritual journey consist of spiritual and ascetic practices *(riyāḍat)* to discipline the soul. Since relinquishing material attachments is very difficult, the traveler *(sālik)* begins to cut the binding chains of attachments to the realm of multiplicity little by little and leaves the world of physical nature *('ālam-i ṭab')* behind.

Hardly before the traveler recovers from the exhaustion of this journey, he enters the intermediate world *(barzakh),* which is the world of psychic multiplicity *(kathrat-i anfusīyah).* Here, he clearly realizes how precious are the treasures that material and external multiplicities have stored within his corporeal nature. These are the same imaginal psychic beings that come into being as a result of the traveler's encounter with and interest in external multiplicities and are considered its outcome and by-products.

These thoughts and preoccupations hinder the traveler's wayfaring and take away his serenity and peace of mind. When he wants to take repose in the remembrance of God for a short while, they besiege him like a deluge and threaten his whole being.

جان همه روز از لگد کوب خیال

وز زیان و سود و از بیم زوال

نی صفا می ماندش نی لطف و فرّ

نی به سوی آسمان راه سفر

A soul trampled by fancy imaginations every day,
on profit and loss, and the fear of downfall,
It shall retain neither purity, nor subtlety, nor light
Nor shall there remain a path for its ascension toward heaven.

It is obvious that the pain and distress caused by psychic multiplicities are more powerful than multiplicities of the physical world. For one can willingly and deliberately retreat and isolate oneself and be saved from disturbance of and encounter with external multiplicities. But one certainly cannot free oneself from the disturbance of temptations and imaginations of the carnal soul, for those enticements always accompany one closely and intimately.

The traveler on the path of the Truth and the wayfarer on the way of sincerity and servanthood to God is not frightened by these enemies. He makes up his mind and, with the help of that Holy Melody,[1] takes the road toward his destination and is determined to leave behind the realm of temptations that is usually called the intermediate world *(barzakh)*. However, the traveler must be very alert and careful lest there remain any of those tempting thoughts in the corners of his heart. Because it is a characteristic of these imaginal [psychic] elements to hide in the most obscured corners of the heart in such a way that the traveler is deceived when he wants to cast them out. He may be fooled to believe that he has freed himself of their evil presence and has been relieved of all remnants of the realm of *barzakh*. But when the traveler reaches the spring of life and wants to quench his thirst from the fountains of wisdom, suddenly they attack him and finish him off with the sword of severity and indignation *(qahr)*.

The example of such a traveler is like that of a person who has filled a pool in his house with water but has not touched it for some time. Therefore, all the dirt and impurities of the water have settled down at the bottom of the pool and the water seems clean and clear to him. He assumes that the clarity and purity of the water is permanent. However, as soon he wants to enter the pool or wishes to wash something in it, suddenly all that dirt and sediment contaminates the clear water again and spots of dirt reappear on the surface. Therefore, through persistent spiritual combat and ascetic practices the traveler must acquire such a degree of certitude and inward peace that imaginal psychic elements are subjugated and cannot disturb his mind when he turns his attention to the Beloved Lord.

When the traveler passes through the realm of physical nature *(ṭabʿ)* and the intermediate world *(barzakh),* he enters the world of spirit *(rūḥ).* Then he passes through some other stages. God willing, we shall describe those stages in detail in the coming pages. Suffice to mention that at this stage the traveler shall witness his own soul *(nafs)* as well as Divine Names and Attributes; and gradually shall reach the station of total annihilation *(fanāʾ-yi kullī)* [in God]. Subsequently, he shall find subsistence *(baqāʾ)* in God where eternal life shall be established for him.

هرگز نمیرد آنکه دلش زنده شد به عشق

ثبت است در جریدهٔ عالم دوام ما

One whose heart is revived by love never shall die,
inscribed is our immortality on the tablet of the Universe. (Ḥāfiẓ)

If one reflects and contemplates on the Qurʾānic verses; one would realize that this principle has been clearly spelled out on several occasions, as God witnesses that those wayfarers martyred on His path are immortal beings:

وَلاَ تَحْسَبَنَّ الَّذينَ قُتِلُوا فِي سَبِيلِ اللَّهِ أمْوَاتًا بَلْ أحْيَاءٌ عِنْدَ رَبِّهِمْ يُرزَقُونَ.

consider not dead those who were killed in the path of God,
nay, they are alive and have their sustenance with their Lord. (3:169)

Elsewhere he states that:

كُلُّ شَيْءٍ هَالِكٌ إلاَّ وَجْهَهُ.

everything is destined to perish save His Image. (28:88)

كُلُّ شَيْءٍ هَالِكٌ إلاَّ وَجْهَهُ.

and,

مَا عِنْدَكُمْ يَنْفَدُ وَمَا عِنْدَ اللَّهِ بَاقٍ.

That which you have shall disappear, and that which is with Allāh remains. (16:96)

If one relates the meaning of these verses, it will become clear that *"those who are alive and have their sustenance with their Lord"* are the Image of God *(wajh Allāh),* which is, as the Holy Qur'ān indicates, eternal and free of degeneration and decadence. In addition, these and other similar verses of the Exalted Qur'ān make it abundantly clear that what is meant by the eternal and imperishable Image of God are, in fact, the Divine Names *(asmā'-i ilāhīyah).* This conclusion is substantiated by exposition in another verse of the Qur'ān where God refers to His Imperishable Image as His Names, which possess attributes of majesty and glory:

كُلُّ مَنْ عَلَيْهَا فَانٍ وَيَبْقَى وَجْهُ رَبِّكَ ذُو الجَلاَلِ وَالإكْرَامِ.

Everyone which is thereon shall pass away, there shall remain but the Majestic and Glorious Image of your Lord. (55:26–27)

All commentators [of the Holy Qur'ān] unanimously agree that in the verse mentioned above the word *possessor (dhū)* stands as the adjective for *Image (wajh)* and means that only the Image of God, which possesses Majesty and Glory, is eternal. Since we know that the image of every possible thing *(shay')* is that which one encounters, therefore, the image of each possible thing is the locus of its manifestation *(maẓhar).* By the same token, the loci of manifestation *(maẓāhir)* of God's Image are through His Names whereby all creatures encounter Him. It follows that all creatures are subject to annihilation and dissolution except Divine Names, which manifest His Majesty and Beauty. Therefore, it becomes clear that those travelers on the path of God who are honored and blessed to attain the noble station of *"living before their Lord and having their sustenance from*

Him," in fact, are manifestations of the Names of Majesty and Beauty of the Lord, Almighty and Exalted is He.

It is in this context that we can understand what the Immaculate Imāms, may God's greetings be upon them, meant when they said, "We are the Names of God/*naḥnu asmā' Allāh.*" (نحن أسماء الله.). Obviously, outward authority over the community by virtue of providing guidance in exoteric affairs or representing the *Sharī'ah* was not such an important function that the Imāms would describe it in such a manner. Rather, such a description depicts the very same station of annihilation in the Unicity of Divine Essence, which is a prerequisite for the Imām to be the Image of God and the most perfect manifestation of His Attributes of Majesty and Beauty; a station that is not comparable with any other function and station.

One of the most important elements of and requirements in the path of wayfaring and spiritual journey is constant attention *(murāqabah).* From the first step that the traveler takes on the Path until the last step, he should never be negligent in observing *murāqabah.* This is one of the absolute necessities for the traveler. It should be known that *murāqabah* consists of various stages and levels. In the early phases of wayfaring, the traveler practices a different kind of *murāqabah* than at later stages. The higher the stages and levels one traverses and the more one advances toward perfection, the more intense and more profound one's *murāqabah* becomes—so much so that if it were to be imposed on a novice in the initial stages of wayfaring, he would not be able to bear it and would abandon wayfaring entirely; or he would be burnt out and consumed by it and perish. However, gradually and as a result of persistence and passing through preliminary stages, the traveler will be strengthened and prepared to enter into higher levels of *murāqabah.* At these stages, many things that were permissible and lawful for him in the early stages become unlawful and forbidden.

As a result of persistent *murāqabah,* gradually signs of affection and love appear in the inmost consciousness of the traveler. Because love for nondelimited [Divine] beauty and perfection *(jamāl wa kamāl 'ala'l iṭlāq)* is primordial to man's nature. It is a treasure that is deposited in man's nature and engraved in his essence. But interest in material possessions and love for multiplicities become a veil for this primordial love and prevents this eternal light from manifesting itself. Through *murāqabah* the veils gradually turn thinner and eventually disappear, and that primordial love manifests itself in one's heart and guides him to that Source of Beauty and Perfection. In the terminology of the gnostics, *murāqabah* is referred to as wine *(mey):*

به پیر میکده گفتم که چیست راه نجات

بخواست جام «می» و گفت راز پوشیدن

I asked the old man of the tavern the path to deliverance,
he called for a cup of wine and said,
"guarding the secrets of [Divine] mysteries"! (Ḥāfiẓ)

and,

راه خلوتگه خاصم بنما تا پس ازین

«می» خورم با تو و دیگر غم دنیا نخورم

Guide me into that special retreat so that from now on
with Thee I may drink sweet wine,
and think no more of the world's bitter woes. (Ḥāfiẓ)

When the traveler carefully persists in his *murāqabah,* God, Exalted is He, out of His love and grace, makes certain lights shine upon him as the first glimmers of gnosis. In the beginning, these lights appear like flashes of lightning and disappear as suddenly as they shine. However, gradually they become stronger, first like a small shining star that grows in brilliance and then turns into the shining Moon and then to the Sun. Sometimes these lights appear like a candle or lantern. In the terminology of gnostics this state and these lights are called gnostic nap *(nawm-i 'irfānī).* These lights are from the category of beings that belong to the intermediary world *(barzakh).*

When the traveler observes the intricacies of *murāqabah* in a consistent and intense manner, and becomes spiritually stronger, these lights also become stronger in such a way that he sees the entire Earth and Heaven, from East to West, totally illuminated. This light is the light of the soul, which appears while passing through the intermediate world *(barzakh).* In the early phases of this stage, when the traveler goes through the intermediate world and the self-disclosure of his soul begins *(tajallīyāt-i nafs),* he sees his soul in a physical material form. In other words, often he might see himself standing before himself. This stage is the beginning of the process of disentanglement of the soul *(tajarrud-i nafs).*

Our teacher and master, the late Ḥājj Mīrzā Āqā Qāḍī, may God be pleased with him, once said, "One day I left my room and went into the verandah, I saw myself standing silently in a corner. I looked very carefully at my face and observed a mole on it. Upon returning to my room, I looked into the mirror and saw a mole on my face that I had not noticed until then."

At times, the traveler feels that he has lost himself and no matter how hard he may seek he does not find himself. As it was mentioned, these visions occur in the preliminary stages of the disentanglement of the soul and are subject to time and space. But later on, with the help of God's grace, the traveler can witness the entire reality of his soul in its totally detached and cathartic state.

An episode has been reported by Ḥājj Mīrzā Jawād Āqā Malikī Tabrīzī who, for fourteen years, was the student and close companion of the late Ākhūnd Ḥusayn Qulī Hamadānī, the master of gnosis and *tawḥīd,* may God be pleased with him. He said that "One day my master assigned the task of training one of his students to me. The student was of high spiritual aspirations and was very determined in his learning. For six years he struggled in constant attention *(murāqabah)* and spiritual combat *(mujāhadah)* until he reached a station which was the station of total capability for understanding and disentangling the soul. I wished that this traveler of the path of salvation receive the grace of initiation at the hands of the Master and be dressed by him in this sacred garb. I took him to the house of our Master and brought up my request. The Master said, 'This is very simple.' Then he made a gesture with his hand and said: 'Disentanglement of the soul is like this.' That student later told me that 'Suddenly, I saw that I had separated from my body and there was someone like myself standing on my side.'"

It should be mentioned that witnessing the beings from the intermediate world *(barzakh)* is not a noble experience or such an honor by itself. Rather, the nobility of that experience is witnessing the soul in its state of complete detachment and perfect catharsis. Because it is at this state that the soul appears in its total detached reality, it can be seen as a being that is not bound by time and space and contains the East and the West in itself. In contrast to earlier visions, this vision is no longer particular, but is in the category of the perception of universal meanings.

Another episode is related by the late Āqā Sayyid Aḥmad Karbalā'ī, may God be pleased with him. He was one of the most prominent and well-known pupils of the late Ākhūnd Ḥusayn Qulī Hamadānī. He said: "One day I was resting in a certain place when somebody woke me up and asked me if I would like to see the Divine Light *(Nūr-i isfahbudīyah)*.[2] When I opened my eyes, I saw an endless light that covered the East and the West of the universe." May God nurture our soul by this light. This phase is the same stage as the self-disclosure of the soul *(tajallī-yi nafs)*, which is seen in this form and in the quality of endless light.

After putting this phase behind and as a result of persistence in *murāqabah*, in accordance with requisites of higher spiritual planes and requirements of those stations, the blessed traveler succeeds in having authentic visions of the Attributes of God, Exalted is He, and understanding the Names of Divine Essence in their totality. At this stage, it may happen that the traveler suddenly realizes that all creatures of the world, in fact, constitute a single body of knowledge. In other words, he may understand that there is no other power, but a Single Power. This occurs at the stage of witnessing Divine Attributes *(shuhūd-i ṣifāt)*. But in the stage of witnessing Divine Names *(shuhūd-i asmā')*, which is still a higher plane than this, the wayfarer realizes that in the entire universe there is but one Knower, one Powerful, and one Living Being. This realization, which takes place at the plane of the heart, is the most noble and most perfect station because the traveler attains a station where he does not see any power, knower, and living being except God, Exalted is He.

لأنَّ السَّالِكَ يُصْبِحُ وَلاَ يَرَى قَادِرًا وَلاَ عَالِمًا وَلاَ حَيًّا سِوَى اللَّه تَعَالَى

> Because the wayfarer *becomes* and does not see any powerful, knowing, and living being except God, Exalted is He.

This realization often takes place during the recitation of the Holy Qur'ān. More often than not, the reciter perceives that someone else, and not he is the reciter. Sometimes he may realize that even the listener has been somebody else and not he.

It should be known that recitation of the Qur'ān plays a great part in reaching this station. It is appropriate for the traveler to recite the chapters *(suwar-i 'azā'im)** while performing the night prayer. Because from the standing position going into prostration before God is not without grace. Experience has shown that the recitation of the blessed *Sūrah Ṣād* (chapter 38) in the one-*rak'ah* [Persian *rak 'at*]prayer *(watīrah)* on Friday night is very efficacious. The special grace of this chapter is clear from the traditions narrated concerning the blessings associated with its recitation.

When the traveler completes these stages with the help of Divine grace and experiences these visions, Divine attractions *(jadhabāt-i illāhīyah)* surround him, and at every moment take him closer to real annihilation until Divine attractions totally take him over and his attention is fixed on nondelimited and Absolute Divine Beauty and Perfection. He forgets [sets on fire] his own existence and all other beings, and will not see anything else before his eyes but the splendid Face of the Beloved; as it has been said:

كَانَ اللّٰهُ وَلَمْ يَكُنْ مَعَهُ شَيْءٌ

God was, and there was nothing else besides Him.

In this state the wayfarer leaves the realm of separation and is immersed in the infinite ocean of witnessing the Lordly Essence of God.[3]

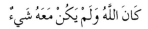

It must be born in mind that wayfaring and spiritual journey is not in contradiction with the traveler's existence in and interaction with the material world. The multiplicity in the external world always remains as it is, and the traveler finds unity within that multiplicity. A prominent [gnostic] once said that "I lived among the people for thirty years. They thought that I was in their company and had constant association with them, whereas throughout this period I did not see or know anybody except God." This is a very important and exalted state *(ḥāl)*, for in the initial stages of wayfaring it may appear occasionally and for a short time, but gradually it becomes more intense, extending for ten minutes or more and then one hour or more, and eventually, with Divine grace, it might pass beyond a state and become a station *(maqām)*. In the tradition and terminology of the people of eminence *(buzurgān)* and people of good deed (*Akhyār* [Qur'ān, 38: 47–48]) this state is referred to as subsistence in the Worshiped One *(baqā' bi ma'būd)*. One cannot reach this station except after total annihilation of his contingent being in the Sacred Essence of the One. In this station the traveler sees nothing except the Sacred Divine Essence.

It has been reported that once there was a certain sage [in Tabrīz] named Bābā Farajullāh who was totally immersed in Divine attraction, hence his title *majdhūb*. When he was asked to describe the worldly life, he replied that "Since I was born [lit. opened my eyes] I have not seen the world so that I can describe it now."[4]

In the early stages of wayfaring, when this kind of vision is not very powerful yet and is independent of the traveler's will, it is called a state *(ḥāl)*. However, as a result of persistence in *murāqabah* and with Divine help it passes from a state and becomes a station *(maqām)*. At this point it comes under his control and will. Obviously, a [spiritually] strong traveler is the one who is conscious of his own state while at the same time is cognizant of the world of multiplicities and conducts the affairs of both with utmost care. This is an exalted and sublime station and is attainable only with great difficulty. Perhaps it is attained only by prophets and Friends of God *(awliyā' Allāh)* and whomever God wills. The Prophet's description of his states can be noticed in such wayfarers when he said:

لِي مَعَ اللَّهِ حَالاَتٌ لاَ يَسَعُهَا مَلَكٌ مُقَرَّبٌ

> Inwardly I have such exalted states with God which no angel brought nigh encompasses,

while outwardly, those states are the example of my human state, as mentioned in the Qur'ān:

أَنَا بَشَرٌ مِثْلُكُمْ

I am only a mortal human being like you. (18:110)

One may argue that these stations are exclusive and attainment to this level of Divine knowledge is solely confined to exalted prophets and infallible *Imāms*—may God's greeting and peace be upon them all—and that others have absolutely no access to it. In response we say that positions of prophethood and imamate are exclusive, but reaching the station of absolute *tawḥīd* and annihilation in the Divine Essence; which is considered the same as *wilāyat* is not exclusive at all. In fact it is to this plane of perfection that prophets and *Imāms,* may Peace be upon them, have called the community of believers. The Noble Messenger, may God bless him and his progeny, called the community of believers *(ummah)* to set their feet on his footstep and reach the plane where he himself stands. This is indicative of the possibility of wayfaring toward that destination; otherwise, the call would have been pointless.

لَقَدْ كَانَ لَكُمْ فِي رَسُولِ اللَّهِ أُسْوَةٌ حَسَنَةٌ لِمَنْ كَانَ يَرْجُوا اللَّهَ وَالْيَوْمَ

الآخِرَ وَذَكَرَ اللَّهَ كَثِيراً

> Verily, in the Messenger of Allāh you have a good example, for him who looketh unto Allāh and the Last Day, and remember Allāh much. (33:21)

It has been narrated by Sunni authorities that [the Prophet, may peace be upon him] said:

لَوْلاَ تَكْثِيرٌ فِي كَلاَمِكُمْ، وَتَمْرِيجٌ فِي قُلُوبِكُمْ لَرَأَيْتُمْ مَا أرَى،

وَلَسَمِعْتُمْ مَا أسْمَعُ.

> Were it not for loquacity of your sayings and temptation and anxiety in your hearts, you would indeed see what I see and hear what I hear.

This statement of the Noble Messenger, may God bless him and his family, indicates clearly that the causes of one's failure to attain human perfection are delusional and satanic thoughts and futile acts. Moreover, it has been reported by Shīʿite authorities that the Prophet said,

لَوْلاَ أنَّ الشَّيَاطِينَ يَحُومُونَ حَوْلَ قُلُوبِ بَنِي آدَمَ لَرَأوْا مَلَكُوتَ السَّمَاوَاتِ وَالأَرْضِ.

> Were it not for the devils surrounding the hearts of the children of Adam, they would witness the Kingdom *(malakūt)* of Heavens and Earth.

One of the signs of this exalted human station is reaching a general comprehension of the Divine realms in accordance with one's talent and preparedness. The result of this comprehension is the knowledge of the past and the future, and control and command over subliminary creatures. Because that which is all-inclusive has total domination over that which it includes. It accompanies everyone and is present everywhere.

Shaykh ʿAbd al-Karīm Jīlī, one of the famous gnostics, writes in his book *al-Insān al-Kāmil*[5] that: "I remember that once for a moment I experienced a state wherein I found myself united with all existents so that they were all directly present before my eyes, but this state did not last for more than a moment." Of course, what prevents the persistence of this state is man's preoccupation with his bodily needs. The complete attainment of this station is possible only after [the soul] abandons its preoccupation with the needs of the body. One of the gnostics of India by the name of Shaykh Walīullāh of Delhi in his book entitled *Hamaʿāt*[6] says: "I was given the knowledge that freedom from the effects of material life takes place five hundred years after death and departing the world of matter." And this period corresponds to one half of a day before the Lord, as the Almighty has said:

وَإِنَّ يَوْماً عِنْدَ رَبِّكَ كَألْفِ سَنَةٍ مِمَّا تَعُدُّونَ.

> And verily a day with thy Lord is like a thousand years in accordance with what you reckon. (The Holy Qur'ān, 22:47)

Of course, it is obvious that other levels and effusions of the Divine Realm are unlimited and unbounded. Since human need is the basis of verbal expression and the scope of verbal expression expands with the growth of his material needs, therefore, description of the realities of the absolute disengaged lights of the Divine realms in ordinary human language is impossible. Whatever can be said about those realms are only indications and allusions and cannot bring the Supreme Reality down to the level of human understanding.

The corporeal human being lives in the world of matter, which is the darkest of all the Divine abodes, as this plain text of tradition clearly indicates:

أنْتَ فِي أظْلَمِ العَوَالِمِ

You are in the darkest of the [Divine] realms.

He invents names and phrases for anything he sees with his eyes and touches with his hands to meet his needs for daily communication. However, he has no knowledge of the other realms of [Divine] light and spirit, nor of their peculiarities, so that he can invent words for them as well. Among all languages of the world there is not a language that can describe those supreme realities and meanings. Therefore, how can one express those realities and describe them in ordinary human language?

مشکل عشق نه در حوصله دانش ماست

حل ابن نکته بدین فکر خطا نتوان کرد

The dilemma of love is not within the reach of our knowledge
By these misguided thoughts one cannot solve this puzzle.

Two groups of people have spoken about these realities. The first group is the noble prophets, may peace be upon them. It is obvious that they had ties with the realms beyond the material world. However, in consideration with the dictum:

> We, [the prophets], have been commanded to speak to the people in accordance with the level of their intellects,
>
> نَحْنُ مَعَاشِرَ الأَنْبِيَاءِ اُمِرْنَا أنْ نُكَلِّمَ النَّاسَ عَلَى قَدْرِ عُقُولِهِمْ.

they had to explain these realities in a manner understandable for common people. For this reason, they refrained from describing the luminous realities and the extent of their brilliance, and abstained from describing issues that never entered the heart of ordinary human beings. For instance, they interpreted those realities that

> No eye had seen, no ear had heard, and had not occurred to any heart
>
> مَا لا عَيْنٌ رَأتْ وَلاَ اُذُنٌ سَمِعَتْ وَلاَ خَطَرَ عَلَى قَلْبِ بَشَرٍ

in such terms as *paradise, beautiful angels, magnificent palaces,* and so on. Ultimately, however, they had to confess that reflection of the realities of those realms cannot be confined in human terms and description.

The second group is a number of individuals who, by following the path of the prophets are blessed and honored with a perception of these realities and Divine effusion in accordance with the degree of their intellect and preparedness. They too have spoken about these realities in analogical and metaphorical terms.

The Realms of Khulūṣ and Ikhlāṣ (Sincerity and Purity)

It should be known that these stages and stations cannot be achieved without sincerity on the path of God. Unless the traveler reaches the station of the Sincere people *(mukhlaṣīn),* the Truth will not be discovered and revealed to him as properly as it should be.

Know that *ikhlāṣ* and *khulūṣ* are of two categories. The first is the sincerity in the worship of and faith in God, the Almighty. The second is sincerity and purity for its own sake. The first is referred to in the following noble verse:

وَمَا أُمِرُوا إلاَّ لِيَعْبُدُوا اللَّهَ مُخْلِصِينَ لَهُ الدِّينَ

And they are not ordained but to serve God, they are sincere before Him. (98:5)

The second point is referred to in the noble verses:

إلاَّ عِبَادَ اللَّهِ الْمُخْلَصِين

. . . except the sincere slaves of God. (37:40, 74, 128, 160)

In addition, the famous tradition *(ḥadīth)* of the Prophet alludes to the second category of sincerity:

مَنْ أخْلَصَ لِلَّه أرْبَعِينَ صَبَاحاً ظَهَرَتْ يَنَابِيعُ الْحِكْمَةِ مِنْ قَلْبِهِ إلَى لِسَانِهِ.

Whoever purifies his soul and his acts for God for forty days, springs of wisdom will flow from his heart toward his tongue.

In other words, only the person who purifies his soul for God, the Exalted, can reach this station.

An explanation to clarify this brief statement is in order. In some verses of the Qur'ān, God, the Exalted, has identified righteousness *(ṣalāḥ)* with *action,* as He says:

مَنْ عَمِلَ صَالِحًا. (16-: 97)

Whoever acts righteously . . .

عَمِلَ عَمَلاً صَالِحاً.

or, Whoever does righteous deeds. . .

and

الَّذينَ آمَنُوا وَعَمِلُوا الصَّالِحَاتِ.

Those who believe and do righteous deeds . . . (2:25)

And in some other verses God attributes righteousness to human essence, as He says in the following verses:

إنَّهُ مِنَ الصَّالِحِينَ.

Verily, he is one of the righteous people. (75:21)

وَصَالِحُ المُؤْمِنِينَ.

and "the righteous of believers . . ." (66:4)

Similarly, purity *(ikhlāṣ)* and sincerity *(khulūṣ)* have been at times attributed to deeds, and at times to human essence. Obviously, realization of purity at the plane of essence is contingent upon its attainment at the plane of action. In other words, unless one reaches the state of total sincerity and purity in his deeds and words, as well as in activity and passivity, he would not attain the stage of purity of essence *(ikhlāṣ-i dhātī)*. God, Exalted is He, has said:

إلَيْهِ يَصْعَدُ الْكَلِمُ الطَّيِّبُ وَالْعَمَلُ الْصَّالِحُ يَرْفَعُهُ.

Unto Him ascend good words, and the righteous act He exalts it. (35:10)

By reference of the pronoun to the subject of the act—"He exalts *(yarfaʿa)* to *the righteous act*"—the verse actually reads:

الْعَمَلُ الْصَّالِحُ يَرْفَعُ الْكَلِمَ الطَّيِّبَ.

Verily the righteous deed exalts good words.

It must be borne in mind that when one reaches this exalted station and attains purity of essence, one will acquire certain traits and characteristics that others lack. First of all, the devil *(shayṭān)* no longer has authority and control over him, as the Noble Qur'ānic ordinance affirms:

فَبِعِزَّتِكَ لأُغْوِيَنَّهُمْ أَجْمَعِينَ إِلاَّ عِبَادَكَ مِنْهُمُ الْمُخْلَصِينَ.

By thy might, I surely will deceive them all, save Thy sincere and pure slaves. (38:83)

It is evident that this exception is not a privilege ordained by the *Sharī'ah*. Rather, it is a prerogative emanating from the *essential* authority of the sincere ones *(mukhlaṣīn)* earned in the station of unity with God *(tawḥīd)* where the devil has no power and cannot reach because of his incapability and weakness.

Since the sincere ones have purified themselves for God, they see God in everything they behold. In whatever manner or form that Satan may appear to them, they see it with Divine eye and treat him with Divine blessing. As a result, Satan admits his helplessness and submits to them. Otherwise, Satan inherently strives to deceive mankind and has no mercy toward anyone, and does not stop seducing and misleading him.

Second, this group will be exempted from reckoning on the day of Resurrection and from attending the scene of judgment. It is mentioned in the Noble Qur'ān:

وَنُفِخَ فِي الصُّورِ فَصَعِقَ مَنْ فِي السَّمَاوَاتِ وَمَنْ فِي الأَرْضِ إِلاَّ مَنْ

شَاءَ اللَّهُ.

And the Trumpet shall be blown, and all those who are in the heavens and the earth shall swoon, save whom God wills. (39:68)

It is safe to conclude with certainty from this verse that there is a group of people who will be immune from fear and horror *(faza' wa ṣa'aqah)* on the day of Resurrection.[7] When one reads that verse in conjunction with the next verse:

فَإِنَّهُم لَمُحْضَرُونَ إِلاَّ عِبَادَ اللَّهِ الْمُخْلَصِينَ.

So they will surely be present, save the sincere slaves of God. (37: 127- 28)

It will be clear that the group which will be exempted from the fear of the day of judgment includes all sincere slaves of God *(mukhlaṣīn).* For the sincere slaves of God, in fact, never commit any act for which they must reckon on the day of judgment. On the contrary, through persistent *murāqabah* and ascetic practices in the struggle against the carnal soul *(jihād-i anfusīyah),* they have died and attained eternal life, and have thus transcended the Greater Resurrection of the soul. Their account has been scrutinized in the course of their spiritual combat *(mujāhadah).* Since they have died in the path of God, they have been dressed in the robe of eternal life before God and enjoy special sustenance from the Divine Treasure. As God, the Exalted has said:

وَلاَ تَحْسَبَنَّ الَّذِينَ قُتِلُوا فِي سَبِيلِ اللَّهِ أَمْوَاتًا بَلْ أَحْيَاءٌ عِنْدَ رَبِّهِمْ يُرْزَقُونَ.

Consider not dead those who were killed in the path of God; Nay, they are alive and have their sustenance with their Lord. (3:169)

Moreover, calling one *(iḥḍār)* [to the presence of God on the day of judgment] implies one's absence [before God]; whereas this group of people *(mukhlaṣīn)* has always been present [before Him], long before the dawn of the day of resurrection, and have been conscious of all states; as God, Exalted is He, has said:

عِنْدَ رَبِّهِمْ يُرْزَقُونَ.

they have sustenance with their Lord.

Third, whatever rewards one may be entitled to and enjoy on the Day of Judgment will be in consideration of one's deeds, save this class of His slaves for whom Divine munificence is far beyond the ordinary reward for acts. As He says:

وَمَا تُجْزَوْنَ إلاَّ مَا كُنْتُمْ تَعْمَلُونَ إلاَّ عِبَادَ اللّٰهِ الْمُخْلَصِينَ.

> You will be rewarded nothing save for what you did, except the sincere slaves of God. (37:39–40)

If it is argued that this verse addresses only those tormented and chastised souls *(mu'adhdhabīn)* who will be rewarded [or punished] in accordance with their acts, and not God's virtuous servants whose reward is not in accordance with their deeds but is based on God's generosity and munificence; we shall say that the meaning of this verse is absolute and is not particularly addressed to the group of the chastised *(mu'adhdhabīn)*. Moreover, God's rewarding His creatures in accordance with His grace and generosity does not preclude [His] rewarding them for their deeds. For the quality of generosity *(faḍl)* implies that the Generous Lord will grant a disproportionately large reward in return for insignificant deeds. In other words, He will consider minor deeds as very important indeed. Nevertheless, rewards will still be in return for one's deeds, whereas the meaning of the noble verse cited above is something else. It means that the sincere servants of God are not at all recompensed in return for their deeds. Also it is stated in another verse that:

لَهُمْ مَا يَشَاؤُنَ فِيهَا وَلَدَيْنَا مَزِيدٌ.

> There they shall have all they desire, and there is more [for them] with Us. (50:35)

As this verse points out, not only shall they [the sincere slaves of God] receive what they desire, there will also be additional rewards for them before God. Hence, it is obvious that they shall receive such gifts of Divine generosity more than what they will or desire and far beyond their imagination or expectation. This is a profound issue that deserves special attention and must always be borne in mind.

Fourth, the sincere *(mukhlaṣīn)* have such a high status and sublime station that permits them to praise God and be grateful to the Supreme Being *in a manner that befits Him (kamā huwa ḥaqquhū)*. God, Exalted is He, has said:

سُبْحَانَ اللَّهِ عَمَّا يَصِفُونَ إِلاَّ عِبَادَ اللَّهِ الْمُخْلَصِينَ

Glorified is God from that which they attribute unto Him,
save what the sincere slaves of God [attribute]. (37:159–160)

This is the ultimate perfection of a creature and the highest possible station one can achieve.

We can conclude from what was discussed thus far the types of privileges and effusions associated with the last station of spiritual journey, which is the station of the *mukhlaṣīn.* However, it should be clear that attainment of these attributes and perfections, and actualization of these realities will not be possible unless the wayfarer dies in the process of spiritual combat *(mujāhadah)* in the path of God. He will become intoxicated by those Divine effusions only when he drinks from the cup of martyrdom. What we mean by *death* and *martyrdom* in this context is, of course, disentanglement of one's soul and its detachment from one's corporeal being and the severance of one's love for bodily attachments and anything associated with it. In the same manner that in the middle of the battlefield a martyr uses his sword to liberate his soul from bodily concerns, the wayfarer too uses his inward sword in the battle against his carnal soul; and with the help of the power of the All-Merciful liberates his spirit from its attachment to his corporeal being.

In the beginning of the spiritual journey, by resorting to asceticism *(zuhd),* contemplation on and awareness of the heedless and transient nature of the world and the futility of attachment to it, the traveler in the path of God should sever the chain of attachment to the world of multiplicity. Since asceticism results in detesting worldly affairs, the wayfarer would not rejoice in occurrences that result in his outward and material gains; neither would he grieve for those events that bring him material loss.

لِكَيْلاَ تَأْسَوْا عَلَى مَا فَاتَكُمْ وَلاَ تَفْرَحُوا بِمَا آتَيكُمْ.

> . . . that you grieve not for the sake of what escapes you, nor rejoice over what you are given. (57:23)

This resignation and lack of longing [for the world] is not in contradiction with feelings of happiness and/or sadness in God. Because this kind of happiness does not derive from the love of wealth, or fame and other contingent affairs; it emanates from one's finding himself immersed in the ocean of Divine munificence and generosity.

After passing through this stage, the traveler will find out that he has a strong interest in and attachment to his own soul and likes himself to the point of extreme love *(ʿishq)*. He will realize that all his efforts and spiritual combat *(mujāhadah)*, in effect, emanate from his excessive love for his own soul. Since a human being is selfish and egocentric by nature; he loves himself and sacrifices everything for the love of his own soul, and does not avoid destroying anything for his own survival. Struggle against self-centeredness and elimination of this natural instinct is the most difficult of all difficult tasks. Unless this passion is totally eliminated and this instinct killed, the light of God will not manifest itself in one's heart. In other words, so long as the traveler does not free himself of himself, he will not join God.

By pleading for Divine Grace and continuous help and mercy of the Most Merciful, the traveler must gradually weaken the ties of self-love and self-centeredness, and eventually sever them all. He must recant this inner idol, which is the source of all vices; and consign it to oblivion once and for all so that all his deeds would be definitely for the sake of Sacred Divine Essence only, and his love for himself would be transformed into the love of God. This can only be attained through spiritual combat.

After traversing this phase and having severed all his ties, the traveler no longer has any attachment to his corporeal being and its needs, even to the bondage of his soul. Now, whatever he does is for God's sake. If he earns a living and obtains means of livelihood to meet his needs to a reasonable extent, it is because his Eternal Beloved wills him to live. Otherwise, he would not take a single step for maintaining this earthly life. Of course, the traveler's desire to live is in verticality with God's Will, and not horizontal and parallel to it. Therefore, he should not expect unveiling (of the Truth) or miracles and take steps to actualize them, nor pray and invoke with the intention to discover invisible things or read minds and mysteries, or acquire such powers as the ability to walk around the earth *(ṭay al-arḍ).* He should not undertake ascetic practices to strengthen and/or display special mental and psychic power in any way and form, because such a person no longer worships God or travels on the path of the Beloved and cannot be sincere. On the contrary, it is his own soul that he worships and whose needs he meets and whose powers he actualizes, although he never confesses with his tongue to this evil act and claims that all his prayers are for God's sake. Such a person is the one who turns his own soul into an object of his worship. He, in fact, worships his whims and desires as the following noble verse of the Qur'ān indicates:

أفرَأيْتَ مَنْ اتَّخَذَ إلٰهَهُ هوَاهُ.

Have you seen him who has made his desire his god? (25:43).

The wayfarer must pass beyond this phase and leave it behind, and abandon his soul which always claims "I-ness" *(anānīyah).* God willing, we shall discuss this issue later.

Ultimately, when the traveler passes beyond this station, he gradually forgets that he once loved himself for the sake of God, the Exalted. He no longer sees his own self or any other face except the Infinite and Eternal Beauty of the Beloved. Gradually he will be drawn into that endless ocean without leaving any sign or trace of himself.

It must be borne in mind that the traveler should be alert in the battle against the carnal soul to assure that he defeats the army of Satan completely, wipes out the temptations of the carnal soul *(āthār-i nafsānīyah),* and removes their roots from the hidden corners of his heart. For if an iota of love for wealth, glory, and status, or for pride, ambition, and self-love remains in his heart, he will never attain perfection.

Often, it has been noticed that many aspirants from among the "perfect men" *(kummālīn)* fail in the battle against the carnal soul and do not reach the station of perfection even after years of ascetic practices *(riyāḍat)* and spiritual combat. The reason for their failure is that the roots of certain traits survive in their hearts, while they imagine that they have completely wiped them out. Consequently, when they face God's trial and are confronted with temptations of the carnal soul and its effects, those roots suddenly bloom and grow, and finally defeat the wayfarer.

Success in overcoming the carnal soul and its forces is contingent upon Divine solicitude and special Grace of the Lord of lords *(Rabb al-arbāb);* for it is not possible to traverse this stage without His special grace and assistance.

It has been reported that one day some pupils found the late Sayyid Baḥr al-ʿUlūm,[8] may God be pleased with him, smiling and in a joyous mood. When they asked him about the reason for his happiness, he replied: "After twenty-five years of spiritual combat, now when I look into my soul I realize that my deeds are no longer ostentatious *(riyāʾī),* and that I have at last succeeded in purifying my deeds." One must reflect deeply on this statement.

It should be reiterated that from the beginning of wayfaring and spiritual journeying up to its final stage, the traveler must observe all precepts of the glorious *Sharīʿah,* and must not violate an iota of the exoteric aspects of Divine Law. Hence, should you come across a person who claims to be a spiritual traveler but who does not observe all rituals and duties set by the *Sharīʿah,* or is not committed to piety and abstention from sin, or deviates even slightly from the straight path of the true *Sharīʿah;* be aware that such a person is a hypocrite *(munāfiq),* unless it is proved that he commits unintended errors or is forgetful.

It has been heard from some people who say that after the wayfarer reaches advanced stations and enjoys Lordly effusions and blessings, he is free from all obligations [to observe the *Sharīʿah*]. This is a prevarication and a false assertion. For even the Prophet, who was the most perfect and noblest of all creation observed all sacred precepts [of the *Sharīʿah*] until the last moments of his life. Therefore, exemption from religious obligations in this sense is false and an inaccurate assertion. But one can interpret this statement in a different manner, which those who make such an assertion do not understand. That is, performing rites and rituals of worship is a means for the human soul to grow to perfection. Man's faculties and capabilities are transformed from potentiality to actuality through his commitment to prayers and observation of rites of worship. Therefore, for those who have not yet actualized all their potentials in every respect, rites and prayers are necessary in their quest for perfection. But for those who have already achieved complete actualization of all their potentials, performance of rites for the sake of perfection and proximity [to God] is no longer relevant. *Rather, for this group of people, observing the Sharīʿah and performing the rites are required precisely because of the very station they have attained.* Hence, when *'Ā'ishah* asked the Blessed Messenger [Peace be upon him] why he bothered to pray so much when God had declared to him:

لِيَغْفِرَ لَكَ اللَّهُ مَا تَقَدَّمَ مِنْ ذَنْبِكَ وَمَا تَأَخَّرَ.

> . . . that God may forgive thee of thy sins that which is past and that which is to come (48:2),

the Prophet (Peace be upon him) replied, "Do you want me not to be a grateful servant for God?" This statement makes it abundantly clear that performance of the rites of worship for some human souls is not for attaining spiritual perfection, but is purely for the sake of expressing gratitude and appreciation to Almighty God.

The states that the wayfarer experiences as a result of constant attention and spiritual struggle, and which occasionally reveal their luminosity and signs to him, are just the beginning of the process to turn those states into [his] second nature *(malakah)*. For the mere occurrence of such experiences and changes of states are not sufficient in themselves. Through persistence in spiritual struggle, the traveler must try to completely eliminate all traces of the lower world that are concealed and hidden within his being. Unless he can identify with the pure souls of the world, attainment to such pure souls' stations will be impossible for him. In fact, the slightest relapse in wayfaring and spiritual struggle would bring the aspirant down again to the lower world. It is to this subtle point that the following noble verse refers:

"وَمَا مُحَمَّدٌ إِلا رَسُولٌ قَدْ خَلَتْ مِن قَبْلِهِ الرُّسُلُ أَفَإِنْ مَاتَ أَوْ قُتِلَ

انْقَلَبْتُمْ عَلَى أَعْقَابِكُم."

> And Muhammad is but a Messenger (the like of whom) have passed away before him. So, should he die or be slain, will you turn back on your heels? (3:144)

Therefore, the traveler must purify his being outwardly and inwardly and cleanse all impurities from the niches and corners of his heart, so that he may enjoy the companionship of the immaculate souls and the association of pure beings of the higher plenum; as the Holy Qur'ān says:

وَذَرُوا ظَاهِرَ الإِثْمِ وَبَاطِنَهُ.

> And renounce the outwardness of sin and the inwardness thereof. (6:120)

Accordingly, the wayfarer should traverse and leave behind all the realms that precede the realm of sincerity *(khulūṣ),* as God, Almighty and Exalted is He, has stated in this blessed verse in an undifferentiated manner:

الَّذِينَ آمَنُوا وَهَاجَرُوا وَجَاهَدُوا فِي سَبِيلِ اللَّهِ بِأَمْوَالِهِمْ وَأَنْفُسِهِمْ أَعْظَمُ دَرَجَةً عِنْدَ اللَّهِ وَأُولَئِكَ هُمُ الْفَائِزُونَ يُبَشِّرُهُمْ رَبُّهُمْ بِرَحْمَةٍ مِنْهُ وَرِضْوَانٍ وَجَنَّاتٍ لَهُمْ فِيهَا نَعِيمٌ مُقِيمٌ خَالِدِينَ فِيهَا أَبَداً إِنَّ اللَّهَ عِنْدَهُ أَجْرٌ عَظِيمٌ.

> Those who believe, and have migrated from their homes and struggled in the path of God with their wealth and their lives are of much greater station before God. These are the triumphant; their Lord gives them good tidings of mercy from Him and acceptance, and Gardens where enduring pleasure will be theirs. There, they will abide forever. Lo! with God there is immense reward. (9:20–22)

According to this verse, there exist four realms that precede the realm of sincerity *(khulūṣ).* They are (1) *Islām,* that is to say, submission [to the Will of God]; (2) *īmān* or faith [in God, His messenger, and the day of judgment] (3) migration *(hijrat)* [in defense of religion and in protest to injustice], and (4) struggle *(jihād)* in the path of God. Since the wayfaring of a traveler on the path of God is the Greater Struggle *(jihād al-akbar)* (as the Prophet said, "We have now turned from the lesser struggle *[jihād al-aṣghar]* toward the Greater Struggle"). The precondition, therefore, for his wayfaring is that his *islām* and *īmān* should, in fact, be the *Greater Islām* and the *Greater īmān*. Only then is he expected to muster his resolution, and with the help of his inner and outer prophets (faculties), set out on this journey and enter the battlefield of spiritual struggle *(mujāhadah)* so that he can achieve the honor of martyrdom on the path of God.

The traveler must be aware of the fact that from the beginning of his journey up to this stage of *jihād* there are many obstacles created by the devil as well as his fellow human beings. But when he attains the honor of martyrdom and passes beyond the realm of *Greater Islām* and *Greater īmān,* and becomes triumphant in the struggle and achieves martyrdom, he stands at the gate of the realms of the *Greatest Islām,* the *Greatest īmān,* the *Greatest Hijrah,* and the *Greatest jihād,* the impediments of which are the Greatest Heresy *(kufr-i aʿaẕam)* and the Greatest Hypocrisy *(nifāq-i aʿaẕam).* The army of Satan no longer has access to this realm and no power over it. Rather, Satan, who is the chief of all devils will personally block the wayfarer's path. Therefore, the traveler must never assume that just because he has passed those realms, he is immune from the perils of the path and has reached his destination. On the contrary, he must be aware that after crossing the preceding realms, if he fails to traverse the Greatest of those realms, he will become a prey of Satan who will prevent him from reaching his ultimate destination. Therefore, the traveler must have high aspirations and spiritual resolve and determination, and should not permit Satan to afflict him with the Greatest Heresy *(kufr-i aʿaẕam)* or the Greatest Hypocrisy *(nifāq-i aʿaẕam).* Rather, after traversing the stages of the *Greatest Islām* and *Greatest īmān,* he must undertake the Greatest Migration *(hijrat-i ʿuẕmā).* By resorting to the Greatest spiritual struggle *(mujāhadah-yi aʿaẕam),* he should pass through the plain of the Greatest Resurrection of the soul *(qīyāmat-i ʿuẕmā-yi anfusīyah)* to enter the realm of the sincere *(mukhlaṣīn).* May God, Exalted is He, grant us this blessing, God willing!

Notes

1. This Divine Melody *(Naghmah-yi Qudsīyah)* refers to the Covenant that was made between God and man before God brought him into

this world. God asked man *"alastu bi rabbikum, qālū balā. Am I not your Lord, They said Yea, verily You Are."* See, the Holy Qur'ān, 7:172. See also Jalāl al-Dīn Rūmī, *Mathnawī*, III:

همچنانکه ذوق آن بانک الست — در دل هو مؤمنی تا حشر هست

هر که خوابی دید از روز الست — مست باشد در ره طاعات مست

As the taste of that call of Alast,
present it is in the heart of every believing man,
whoever had a dream of the Day of alast,
drunken he will be on the path of obedience and prayers.

2. *Nūr-i Isfahbudīyah:* The Light of lights that is present in the center of man's being. Suhrawardī identifies it with Muhammadān Spirit *(rūḥ-i muḥammadī)* or the Holy Spirit *(rūḥ al-Qudus). Nūr-i isfahbudī* illuminates everything and makes visions possible. Everything that exists in the corporeal existence of the human being is a shadow from that which exists in the *nūr-i isfahbud*. On Suhrawardī and his school see Seyyed Hossein Nasr, *Three Muslim Sages* (New York, 1969); Mahdī Amīn Razavi, *Suhrawardī and the School of Illumination* (New York, 1997), Hossein Zīa'ī', "Shihāb al-Dīn Suhrawardī: founder of the Illuminationist school" in Seyyed Hossein Nasr and Oliver Leaman (eds.), *History of Islamic Philosophy* (London, 1996), vol. 1, chaps. 28 and 29. See also Suhrawardī, *ḥikmat ul-ishrāq*, edited with an introduction and comments by S. J. Sajjādī (Tehran, 1377/1998), 6th ed., and G. I. Dīnānī, *Shu'ā'-i andīshah va shuhūd-i suhrawardī* (Tehran, 1376/1997).

   Suwar-i azā'im are those chapters which require the reciter to prostrate at the end of certain verses. They include chapters 13, 16, 17, 19, 22, 25, 27, 32, 38, 41, 53, 84, and 96.
3. To this *ḥadīth* Sufi's usually add, *Now it is as it has always been (al'ān kamā kān.)* Quoted from Seyyed Hossein Nasr. الآن كما كان.
4. The biographical account of *Bābā Faraj Majdhūb* is available in *Tārīkh-i Ḥashrī*, written on accounts of sages and gnostics of Tabrīz. His sayings, including this one, have been cited in the form of poetry in that book:

که فرج تا که دیده بکَشادست

چشم او بر جهان نیفتاد ست

Since the day Faraj was born into this world (lit. opened his eyes), his eyes have never seen the world.

Ḥāfiẓ also has written a similar poem:

منم که شهرهٔ شهرم به عشق ورزیدن

منم که دیده نیالوده ام به بد دیدن

I am the one who is famed in town for philandering, yet
I am the one who never tainted eyes by seeing wretchedness

Ibn al-Fāriḍ has said:

وَحَيَاةِ أَشْوَاقِي إِلَيْكَ وَتُرْبَةِ الصَّبْرِ الْجَمِيلِ

مَا اسْتَحْسَنَتْ عَيْنِي سِوَاكَ وَلاَ صَبَوْتُ إِلَى خَلِيلِ

My life: my longing for thee,
and my grave: my patience fair,
Beyond thee, my eyes found no charm,
my heart any repose in a friend.

Ibn al-Fāriḍ is reported to have said that he composed this couplet in a dream.

5. ʿAbd al-Karīm Jīlī, *al-Insān al-Kāmil,* Cairo, 1304/1884. Sections of this treatise were translated into English by Arnold Nicholson and published in *Studies in Islamic Mysticism,* Cambridge, 1919. Other parts are available in French translation by Titus Burckhardt, *De l'homme universal,* Lyon, 1952. See Martin Lings, *What Is Sufism,* 2d. ed., 1995.
6. Shaykh Walīullāh of Dihlī was born in 1114/1703 in Delhī and died there in 1176/1762. He was the most prominent Sufi scholar of India and wrote on a variety of subjects including Islamic law, philosophy,

and theology. His biographer states that more than fifty of his works have been published. His most important contributions include *Kitāb al-Hama'āt, Alṭāf al-quds, Ḥujjat Allāh al-Bālighah, Lama'āt,* and *Shifā' al-Qulūb.* See Ḥāfiẓ A. Ghaffār Khān, "Islamic Philosophy in the Modern Islamic World: India," in Nasr and Leaman (eds.), *History of Islamic Philosophy,* Part II, pp. 1051–1075.

7. Holy Qur'ān, 21:103.
8. Sayyid Mahdī ibn Ḥasan ibn Muhammad (1155–1212/1742–1797), one of the most eminent Shī'ite scholars and the author of *al-ijtihād: uṣūluhū wa aḥkāmuhū,* Beirut, 1977, and *Bulghat al-faqīh,* Tehran, 1984.

3

Description of the Realms Preceding the Realm of *Khulūṣ*

As we stated before, the traveler on the path of God, Exalted is He, must traverse twelve realms before entering the realm of *khulūṣ*. These include: the realms of the Lesser, the Greater, and the Greatest submission *(islām-i aṣghar, islām-i akbar,* and *islām-i a'aẕam);* the worlds of the Lesser, the Greater, and the Greatest faith *(īmān-i aṣghar, īmān-i akbar,* and *īmān-i a'aẕam);* the worlds of the Lesser, the Greater, and the Greatest migration *(hijrat-i ṣughrā, hijrat-i kubrā,* and *hijrat-i 'uẕmā);* and finally, the realms of the Lesser, the Greater, and the Greatest spiritual struggle *(jihād-i aṣghar, jihād-i akbar,* and *jihād-i a'aẕam).* Therefore, one must know the peculiarities of these realms and their qualities and effects, characteristics, and signs; and be aware of the impediments and obstacles on the road toward them. Here we shall describe these stages briefly and in an undifferentiated manner, because they have been described in a differentiated manner in the celebrated book attributed to the late *Sayyid Mahdī Baḥr al-'Ulūm,* the pride of all jurists and friends of God, may He place him in His Paradise.[1] Those who seek to learn about it in detail should refer to the work itself. However, for the sake of clarification of the issues, we shall describe them briefly in the coming pages.

The Greater Islām (Islām-i Akbar)

Islām-i akbar consists of total submission and absolute surrender before God, that is to say, renunciation of all complaints and objections before Him, Almighty and Glorious is He. It [also] connotes the recognition of the fact that anything that exists, or any event that takes place, is destined [by God] and, therefore, good; and that which does not occur is not in one's best interest. In short, *Islām-i akbar* calls for total abstinence from questioning and complaining in regard to the Almighty Lord. *Amīr al-Mu'minīn 'Alī,* the Master of all monotheists *(mawlā al-muwaḥḥidīn),* may peace be upon him, described this station in the famous ḥadīth narrated by *Marfū'ah Barqī*[2] in his collection *(Maḥāsin)* in the following terms:

إِنَّ الإِسْلاَمَ هُوَ التَّسْلِيمُ، وَالتَّسْلِيمُ هُوَ الْيَقِينُ.

> Verily, *Islām* means submission *(taslīm),* and submission means certainty *(yaqīn).*

In addition, there should not be any kind of grudge or ill feeling left in the wayfarer's heart toward God's injunctions, whether they pertain to *Sharī'ah* or to God's engendering Command, as indicated in this statement of God, Exalted is He:

فَلاَ وَرَبِّكَ لا يُؤْمِنُونَ حَتَّى يُحَكِّمُوكَ فِيمَا شَجَرَ بَيْنَهُمْ ثُمَّ لا يَجِدُوا

فِي أَنْفُسِهِمْ حَرَجاً مِمَّا قَضَيْتَ وَيُسَلِّمُوا تَسْلِيماً.

> Nay, by thy Lord, they shall not believe (in truth) until they make you judge of what is in dispute between them and find in their hearts no dislike or ill feeling about that which you decide, and submit with full submission. (4:65)

This station is the same as the station of *īmān-i akbar,* wherein *islām-i akbar* has penetrated into the wayfarer's soul and has truly taken over his heart and spirit.

The Greatest Faith (Īmān-i Akbar)

When the heart of the traveler is illuminated with the light of *islām-i akbar,* occasionally a state descends upon him and enables him to witness—in addition to perceiving God's presence intuitively and intellectually—that all that exists is Divinely ordained and supported, Exalted is He. In other words, he finds that God is present and witnessing all things in all circumstances. This is the same as the station of direct vision and the Greater Islām. However, since this state has not yet reached its utmost perfection to take over the wayfarer's total being and take charge of his entire corporeal existence, material obstacles such as natural and ordinary physical preoccupations may distract him from that state. As a result of involvement with these affairs, he may lose [the state of] direct witnessing and vision, and may be taken over by forgetfulness and negligence *(ghaflat,* Arabic *ghaflah).* Therefore, the traveler must remain steadfast and determined and transform that state into a second nature *(malakah)* to attain perfection so that outward preoccupations could not capture him and distract him from the course of *vision (shuhūd).* In other words, he must extend this state *(Islām-i akbar)* from the plane of the heart to that of the spirit until that transient and undifferentiated *(ijmāl)* state is transformed into a differentiated *(tafṣīl)* one and, under the command of the spirit, expand and take over all his manifest and nonmanifest faculties, changing from a passing state and becoming a second nature to him. This is the same station that gnostics/*ʿurafāʾ* call *iḥsān,* as God, the Munificent, states in the Glorious Qurʾān:

وَالَّذِينَ جَاهَدُوا فِينَا لَنَهْدِيَنَّهُمْ سُبُلَنَا

> And those who struggle in Us, We surely guide them to Our paths. (29: 69)

He does not stop here but adds:

وَإِنَّ اللَّهَ لَمَعَ الْمُحْسِنِينَ

> And verily God is with those who do good deeds *(muḥsinīn).*

Therefore, as long as the struggler in the path of God *(mujāhid fī sabīl Allāh)* does not attain the station of *iḥsān,* he will not be able to reach the path of Divine guidance. When the Prophet of Allāh was asked about the meaning of *iḥsān,* He replied:

الإِحْسَانُ أَنْ تَعْبُدَ اللَّهَ كَأَنَّكَ تَرَاهُ، وَإِنْ لَمْ تَكُنْ تَرَاهُ فَإِنَّهُ يَرَاكَ

Iḥsān is to adore Allāh as though thou didst see Him, and if thou dost not see Him, He nonetheless seeth thee.[3]

In other words, one should worship God as though one sees Him. If one is not able to worship Him in this manner, at least he should worship God as if He sees him.

As long as the station of *islām-i akbar* of the traveler does not reach the plane of *īmān-i akbar,* only occasionally does he experience the state of *iḥsān* wherein he performs rites of worship eagerly and with utmost fervor. But when he reaches the realm of *īmān-i akbar,* his state of *iḥsān* is transformed into a second nature and he attains the station of the people of good deeds *(muḥsinīn).* At this point, every conduct and act of the traveler, whether major and significant or minor and insignificant, emanates from his spiritual yearning *(shawq)* and longing *(raghbat,* Arabic *raghbah),* and is carried out with certainty and serenity. Because at this stage faith has taken over the wayfarer's spirit, and since the spirit is the sovereign ruler and commander of all parts and organs of his corporeal being, it employs all of them for its own purpose and facilitates their functions. They all become submissive and obedient to the spirit and do not rebel against it even for a short moment. Concerning people at this station, God, Blessed and Exalted is He, says:

قَدْ أَفْلَحَ الْمُؤْمِنُونَ الَّذِينَ هُمْ فِي صَلَوَتِهِمْ خَاشِعُونَ وَالَّذِينَ هُمْ عَنِ اللَّغْوِ مُعْرِضُونَ.

Prospered indeed are the believers. Those who are humble in their prayers, and who turn away from vain conversation. (23:1–3)

Since preoccupation with illusory and worthless things is derived from a natural inclination and attraction toward them, the traveler who has faith in *īmān-i akbar* and has reached the station of *iḥsān* has no attraction or inclination toward such things. Moreover, he knows that two loves cannot exist in one heart, in accordance with the statement of God, Exalted is He:

مَا جَعَلَ اللَّهُ لِرَجُلٍ مِنْ قَلْبَيْنِ فِي جَوْفِهِ.

God has not placed two hearts in a man's breast. (33:4)

If there is still any inclination in the traveler's heart toward vain matters, we can easily and immediately find out that his heart is devoid of yearning for the Divine, as causes are inferred from their effects. Such a heart would be a hypocritical one, because, on the one hand, it expresses eagerness in matters relating to God, Exalted is He, and on the other hand, it is still preoccupied with vanities and frivolities. This kind of hypocrisy is the Greater Hypocrisy *(nifāq-i akbar),* which stands in sharp contrast to *īmān-i akbar.* Submission and obedience in the heart of such a wayfarer does not emanate from inward yearning and eagerness for God; rather, it is based on fear, caution, and intellectual considerations intuitive to human beings. It is to this hypocrisy *(nifāq)* that this statement of God Almighty refers:

وَإِذَا قَامُوا إِلَى الصَّلَوٰةِ قَامُوا كُسَالَى.

And when they stand for prayer they perform it lackadaisically. (4:142)

The traveler attains the station of *īmān-i akbar* only after he is totally freed from all degrees of hypocrisy *(nifāq)* and when his actions are purely inspired and motivated by love and yearning [for God] and are not based on fear or inspired by prudence, mere intellectual perception, or caution.

The Greater Migration (Hijrat-i Kubrā)

When the traveler arrives at the station of *īmān-i akbar,* he must prepare to make the Greatest Migration *(hijrat-i kubrā).* The Greatest Migration is one's distancing of oneself physically from people who rebel against God, avoiding the company of people who are disobedient to Him *(ahl-i baghy wa ṭughyān),* and people who are preoccupied with the treacherous world.[4]

It is also distancing one's heart from love and attraction toward those people. This migration is as much physical as it is spiritual; it is carried out by one's corporeal being as well as one's soul. It is one's migration and distancing oneself from conventional habits and customs, contingent affairs, rules, and practices that stand in the traveler's path to God and prevent him from advancing. For habits and customs are among the most important elements of the realm of heresy and disbelief.

In a materialistic society, man is delimited by habits and customs based on imagination and sensory intuition *(wahmī),* which the people of the world are accustomed to and upon which they base their gain and loss, as well as their relationships, transactions, and communication with others. For instance, [in such a society] it is usually assumed that someone who sits silently in a scholarly gathering or debate, is ignorant. Or, it has become a habit that people show incoherence in where they sit in a gathering; and in an assembly one's rank and status is determined by where one sits. The same holds true of one's walking ahead of others while entering or leaving a gathering. Adulation and fawning are considered evidence of cordiality, courtesy, and beauty of character, while the opposite of them are regarded as signs of low character, triviality, and ill-naturedness or as the absence of nobility of character and eminence. The traveler must abandon all these illusive habits and with Divine succor migrate from this realm of imagination and sensory intuition, and divorce this old hag once and for all.[5] In the course of this dissociation, the wayfarer must have no concern or fear, nor should he be afraid of the people's adverse opinion, or pay attention to the blame of those who claim knowledge and wisdom. As a *ḥadīth* of the Blessed Prophet narrated by *Imām Ṣādiq* and quoted in [Muhammad ibn Ya'qūb] al-Kulaynī's[6] compendium on the authority of [Ismā'īl ibn Zayd] al-Sukūnī[7] clearly states:

أَرْكَانُ الْكُفْرِ أَرْبَعَةٌ: الرَّغْبَةُ وَالرَّهْبَةُ وَالسُّخْطُ وَالْغَضَبُ.

The pillars of heresy *(kufr)* are four: desire, fear, anger, and rage.

Fear in this context has been interpreted as fearing the people for opposing and violating their customs and norms based on sensory intuition. In short, the traveler must abandon and free himself of all conventional social customs, manners, and contingent affairs that create obstacles [for his journey] on the path of God. The gnostics refer to this attitude as madness *(junūn)* because an insane person is not acquainted with people's customs and habits, nor does he observe or attach any significance to them. He is indifferent to their praise and blame and has no fear of their hostile reaction against him, nor does he try to mend his ways and manners.

ای دل آن به که خراب ازمی کَلکون باشی
بی زر و کَنج به صد حشمت قارون باشی

در مقامی که صدرات به فقیران بخشند
چشم دارم که به جاه ازهمه افزون باشی

تاج شاهی طلبی کَوهر ذاتی بنما
ارخو از کَوهر جمشید وفریدون باشی

کاروان رفت و تو درخواب وبیابان درپیش
کی روی ره زکه پرسی چکنی چون باشی

نقطهٔ عشق نمودم به توهان سهومکن
ورنه چون بنکَری از دائره بیرون باشی

ساغری نوش کن و جرعه برافلاك نشان
تا به چند از غم ایّام جکَر خون باشی ؟

O my heart, better that
you be ruined by rosy wine
And have a glory a hundred times that of Korah,
without his gold and treasure.
In the station where they grant
to the *people of poverty* the position of a king,
I expect that you will find a majesty

superior to all.
If you wish the royal crown,
show the jewel of your essence,
If your jewel is of the same essence as
Faraydūn's and Jamshīd's.
The caravan has departed
and you are asleep,
Ahead lies the desert, When will you set out?
Whom will you ask the way?
What will you do? How will you be?
I have shown you the center of love
so do not falter,
An outsider to the circle you will be
before you shall notice.
Take a cup, and spurt out a sip at the heavens,
How long will you grieve for the world's sorrows.

The Greater Spiritual Struggle (Jihād-i Akbar)

When the traveler, with the help of Lordly providence, succeeds in completing the migration and liberates himself from society's customs and habits, he enters the station of the Greater Spiritual Struggle *(jihād-i akbar).* This is the station of battle against the armies of Satan, because at this stage the wayfarer becomes a captive in the realm of his nature and his sensory intuition, wrath, and lust. He will be captured by conflicting passions, will be surrounded by the darkness of expectations and desires, will be taken over by anxieties and sorrows and anguished by contradictory thoughts and conflicting desires, and constantly expects frightening events. From every corner of his chest a fire attacks him; he constantly worries about poverty and need. His inward being is crushed by conflicting pains and vengeance. At times he is torn apart in the tussles of family and children, while at other times he is fearful of losing wealth and belongings. At times he seeks status but fails to attain it, or pursues power that he fails to earn. The thorns of jealousy, anger, pride, and desires torment him. He becomes a despicable and contemptible victim in the claws of the scorpions and predators of the material and natural world. The abode of his heart becomes tainted by the dark and countless shadows of delusions. Wherever he turns, he is battered by the fist of fate, and wherever he steps thorns will injure his feet.

These pains and illnesses accumulate in the traveler's chest and after much contemplation and consideration, he realizes that they are multifarious. With God's help and grace, the traveler must defeat the armies of sensory intuition, indignation, and lust, and achieve triumph in this greatest spiritual combat *(mujāhada-yi kubrā).* Only after gaining victory in this struggle and freeing himself from the claws of mundane attachments and removing the hurdles from his way, will the wayfarer finally leave the realm of nature behind and bid farewell to it.

The Greatest Submission (Islām-i A'aẕam)

In such a state the traveler enters the realm of *islām-i a'aẕam.* Here, he sees himself like a unique jewel and an unrivaled treasure, encompassing the world of nature, immune from death and annihilation, and free from quarreling with contradictories. He observes within himself a purity, a glory, and an illuminating light that is beyond the perception of the natural world. That is because in this state the traveler has died to the natural world and has found a new life. Although outwardly he lives in the realm of the terrestrial and visible kingdom *('ālam-i mulk wa nāsūt),* he beholds terrestrial *(nāsūtī)* beings in their Heavenly *(malakūtī)* forms. Everything from the material world that he may encounter, he will see in their Heavenly forms; and therefore, they do not disturb him. For he has reached the station of Intermediate Resurrection of the Soul *(qiyāmat-i anfusīya-yi wusṭā),* where veils are removed [before his eyes] and many mysteries are revealed to him, and he experiences many wondrous states. This is the very same station of *islām-i a'aẕam* mentioned clearly in the verses of the Qur'ān:

أَوَ مَنْ كَانَ مَيْتاً فَأَحْيَيْنَاهُ وَجَعَلْنَا لَهُ نُوراً يَمْشِي بِهِ فِي النَّاسِ كَمَنْ مَثَلُهُ

فِي الظُّلُمَاتِ لَيْسَ بِخَارِجٍ مِنْهَا كَذَلِكَ زُيِّنَ لِلْكَافِرِينَ مَا كَانُوا

يَعْمَلُونَ.

> Why is he who was dead, and We have raised him unto life, and set for him a light to walk by among the people, as one who is in darkness whence he can never emerge? So is their conduct made to appear pleasant and fair to the disbelievers. (6:122)

And similarly in the following statement God, the Exalted, has said:

مَنْ عَمِلَ صَالِحاً مِنْ ذَكَرٍ أَوْ أُنْثَى وَهُوَ مُؤْمِنٌ فَلَنُحْيِيَنَّهُ حَيَوةً طَيِّبَةً

وَلَنَجْزِيَنَّهُمْ أجْرَهُمْ بِأحْسَنِ مَا كَانُوا يَعْمَلُونَ.

> Whosoever does righteous deeds, whether male or female, and is a believer, verily We shall revive them with good life, and We shall reward them a recompense in proportion to the best of what they did. (16: 97)

It should be made clear that at this juncture and as a result of what the traveler witnesses in his soul, he may be taken over by pride and I-ness *(anānīyah).* He may encounter his biggest and staunchest enemy, which is nothing but his own carnal soul *(nafs),* as it has been pointed out in this tradition:

أعْدَى عَدُوِّكَ نَفْسُكَ الَّتِي بَيْنَ جَنْبَيْكَ.

> Your most ardent enemy is your carnal soul, which dwells between your two sides.

If the Lordly grace *('ināyāt-i rabbānīyah)* does not save him at this stage, he will be afflicted with the greatest heresy *(kufr-i a'ẕam).* It is this heresy which is referred to in the famous saying:

اَلنَّفْسُ هِيَ الصَّنَمُ الأكْبَرُ.

> The carnal soul is the biggest idol.

Abraham (may peace be upon him) took refuge in God from this kind of heresy and begged Him deliverance from it:

وَاجْنُبْنِي وَبَنِيَّ أَنْ نَعْبُدَ الأَصْنَامَ.

And turn me and my sons away from serving idols. (14:35)

It is quite obvious that heresy in the ordinary sense of the term, that is to say worshiping man-made idols, is inconceivable for a prophet like Abraham who is honored with the glorious title of the Friend of the All-Beneficent *(Khalīl al-Raḥmān).* It was this polytheism from which the Noble Prophet of Islām, may God's blessing and peace be with him, sought refuge in God with this prayer:

اَللَّهُمَّ إِنِّي أَعُوذُ بِكَ مِنَ الْشِّرْكِ الْخَفِيِّ.

O God, I seek Thy refuge from hidden polytheism *(shirk al-khafy).*

In short, the traveler should affirm, with Divine help, his nothingness, admit his helplessness, weakness, lowliness, and slavehood and cast away egotism so that he will not fall victim to the Greatest heresy *(kufr-i a'aẓam),* and can attain the station of the Greatest Islām *(islām-i a'aẓam).* Some of the most celebrated sages among the gnostics would never utter the words "I" and "we" throughout their lives. Instead, they would say, for instance, "This servant *(bandah)* came" and "This servant *(bandah)* left." Some others, in describing their actions, would attribute to God that which was good and derived from Divine Essence, and attribute to themselves that which could not be attributed to Divine Being. And in cases where some deeds could be related to themselves as well as to God they would say "we." They based this practice on the episode of *Khiḍir* and Moses, may Peace be upon them, where *Khiḍir* says:

أَمَّا السَّفِينَةُ فَكَانَتْ لِمَسَاكِينَ يَعْمَلُونَ فِي الْبَحْرِ فَأَرَدْتُ أَنْ أَعِيبَهَا.

> As for the ship, it belonged to certain poor men, who toiled upon the sea; and I desired to mar it. (18:79)

Since inflicting damage may not be attributed to the Divine Essence, Khiḍir attributes that to himself and, hence, uses the proper singular pronoun. However, because the killing [of the lad] could be attributed to Khiḍir and to God, he describes it in the plural.

وَأَمَّا الْغُلَامُ فَكَانَ أَبَوَاهُ مُؤْمِنَيْنِ فَخَشِينَا أَنْ يُرْهِقَهُمَا طُغْيَاناً وَكُفْرا

فَأَرَدْنَا أَنْ يُبْدِلَهُمَا رَبُّهُمَا خَيْراً مِنْهُ زَكَوةً وَأَقْرَبَ رُحْماً.

> As for the lad, his parents were believers; and we were afraid lest he would oppress them by rebellion and disbelief. And we desired that their Lord should change him for them for one better in purity and nearer to mercy. (18:80–81)

On the other hand, since concern for the good, perfection, and usefulness depends on the support of God's Essence, he attributes that to God, the Sustainer:

وَأَمَّا الْجِدَارُ فَكَانَ لِغُلَامَيْنِ يَتِيمَيْنِ فِي الْمَدِينَةِ وَكَانَ تَحْتَهُ كَنْزٌ لَهُمَا

وَكَانَ أَبُوهُمَا صَالِحاً فَأَرَادَ رَبُّكَ أَنْ يَبْلُغَا أَشُدَّهُمَا وَيَسْتَخْرِجَا كَنْزَهُمَا.

> And as for the wall, it belonged to two orphan lads in the city, and there was beneath it a treasure which belonged to them. Their father was a righteous man, and thy Lord intended that they should come to their full maturity and should bring forth their treasure as a mercy from their Lord. . . . (18:82)

The same manner of speech can be observed in the words of Abraham, may peace be upon him, when he said:

الَّذِي خَلَقَنِي فَهُوَ يَهْدِينِ وَالَّذِي هُوَ يُطْعِمُنِي وَيَسْقِينِ وَإِذَا مَرِضْتُ

فَهُوَ يَشْفِينِ.

. . .[He]Who created me and Himself guides me; who Himself feeds me and waters me, and, whenever I am sick heals me. (26:78–80)

Here he attributes sickness to himself and healing to God.

Achieving the station of *islām-i aʿaẕam* and deserting the I-ness of the soul *(rafḍ-i anānīyat-i nafs)* whence Satan resides is possible only with God's grace and providence. Ḥājj Imām-Qulī Nakhjawānī, who taught esoteric sciences to the late Āqā Sayyid Ḥassan Āqā Qāḍī, the father of Āqā Ḥājj Mīrzā ʿAlī Āqā Qāḍī, may God be pleased with them—studied ethics and theology under the tutelage of the late Āqā Sayyid Quraysh Qazwīnī, may God be pleased with him.[8] Ḥājj Imām Qulī traversed stations of perfection in ethics and esoteric sciences and once said: "When I reached old age and was debilitated, I saw myself and Satan as the two of us stood at the peak of a mountain. I pointed to my beard and told him that I am old and dilapidated and asked him to spare me and leave me alone. Satan asked me to look over where he was pointing. When I looked around, I saw a very deep valley so frightening that it could petrify any man's intellect. Satan said, 'There is no mercy or compassion placed in my heart. If I can ever get my hands on you, your place will be at the bottom of this valley that you see!' "

The Greatest Faith (Īmān-i Aʿaẕam)

The station above the Greatest Islām *(islām-i aʿaẕam)* is that of the Greatest Faith *(īmān-i aʿaẕam)*. It is the most intense and exalted expression and manifestation of *islām-i aʿaẕam* when the traveler goes beyond the planes of knowledge and faith and enters the realm of unveiling and direct witnessing *(mushāhadah)*. At this station the wayfarer leaves the realm of the Angelic Kingdom *(malakūt)*, the Greater Resurrection of the Soul *(qiyāmat-i kubrā-yi anfusīyah)* descends upon him, and he enters the realm of Divine Power and Invincibility *(jabarūt).* Thus, after experiencing the vision of the Angelic Kingdom *(malakūt),* he attains the vision of Divine Might and Invincibility *(muʿāyināt-i jabarūtīyah).*

The Greatest Migration (Hijrat-i ʿUẕmā)

After completing the stages mentioned above, the traveler must migrate from his own being, and renounce and abandon it once and for all. This is the journey to the world of Absolute Being *(wujūd-i muṭlaq).* The following statement attributed to a prominent sage points to this stage:

دَعْ نَفْسَكَ وَتَعَالَ.

Say farewell to your *self* and come.[9]

Also God, Exalted is He, refers to this stage in the following verse:

فَادْخُلي فِي عِبَادِي وادْخُلي جَنَّتِي.

. . . And Enter among My servants and enter My Garden.[10] (89: 29–30)

As it is clear, one enters the Divine Garden only after one has already entered the circle of God's servants. The statement:

يَا أيَّتُهَا النَّفْسُ المُطْمَئِنَّةُ.

O thou soul at peace! (89:29)

addresses a soul that has successfully completed the Greater Struggle and has entered the abode of victory and triumph that is the world of tranquillity and peace. However, since such a soul has not yet gone through the Greatest Spiritual combat *(mujāhada-yi ʿuẕmā),* traces of his existence still remain; and their ultimate elimination depends on actualization of the Greatest Spiritual Combat *(jihād-i aʿaẕam)*. Hence, the soul is not yet freed of its own domination and control, and still resides in the expanse of the King *(malīk)* and the Mighty *(muqtadir)*, which are two of the Names of God Almighty:

فِي مَقْعَدِ صِدْقٍ عِنْدَ مَلِيكٍ مُقْتَدِرٍ.

Firmly established in the favor of a Mighty King. (54:55)

After this phase, the traveler must challenge and fight against the remaining weak aspects of his being that still lay hidden in his soul and eliminate them once and for all so that he can enter into the plane of Absolute Unity *(tawḥīd-i muṭlaq)*. This station is the abode of victory. It is in this manner that the twelvefold abodes are traversed. Such a traveler who has completed the Greatest Migration *(hijrat-i ʿuẕmā)* and the Greatest Struggle *(jihād-i aʿaẕam)* triumphantly, will enter the abode of sincerity *(khulūṣ)*. The Greatest Resurrection of the Soul *(qiyāmat-i ʿuẕmā-yi anfusīyah)* will descend upon him and, as the Qur'ān mentions, he shall enter the realm of sincerity and purity *(khulūṣ)* and shall step into the expanse of:

إِنَّا لِلَّهِ وَإِنَّا إِلَيْهِ رَاجِعُونَ.

Verily, we are from God, and, verily, unto Him
we shall return. (2:156)

Such a wayfarer has passed beyond the realms of corporeal and psychic existence, and all other entifications *(taʿayyunāt)*, and has died to them all. He has thus left behind the abode where

كُلُّ نَفْسٍ ذَائِقَةُ الْمَوْتِ.

every soul shall taste death (3:18)

and entered the realm of Divine Names *(Lāhūt).* Such a person will die a voluntary death. The Prophet of Allāh called Imām 'Alī ibn Abī Ṭālib the archetype of such a wayfarer as he said:

مَنْ أَرَادَ أَنْ يَنْظُرَ إِلَى مَيِّتٍ يَمْشِي فَلْيَنْظُرْ إِلَى عَلِيِّ بْنِ أَبِي طَالِبٍ.

Whoever wishes to see a walking dead man, he should look at 'Alī ibn Abī Ṭālib.

Elaboration and Explanation

The stations of perfection that have been mentioned and whose characteristics and qualities have been described briefly thus far are effusions emanating from the Almighty Lord that are exclusive to the *ummah* of the Seal of the Prophets and Apostles, Muhammad ibn 'Abdullāh, may Allāh bless him and his progeny. Perfections attained by wayfarers of previous nations *(umam-i sālifah)* and past religions *(sharāyī'-i māḍiyah)* were, in fact, very limited. After attaining the station of annihilation, they were only able to witness God's Names and Attributes but could not think of a higher station. The mystery to this limitation was that the ultimate achievement of their gnosis *(ma'rifah)* was realization of the Truth contained in *"lā ilāha ill'allāh" (There is no god but Allāh),*

لاَ إِلَهَ إِلاَّ اللَّهُ.

the effects of which leads one to witness the Divine Essence that encompasses only all Attributes of His Perfection and Beauty. But wayfarers of the *ummah* of the Noblest Messenger have gone far beyond this station and have realized subsequent stations that cannot be described or defined. The reason is that all injunctions and precepts of Islām point to the fact that

اللَّهُ أَكْبَرُ مِنْ أَنْ يُوصَفَ.

Allāh is greater than that which can be described.

Based on this fact, stations traversed by a Muslim traveler inevitably lead to a point that cannot be explained or contained in ordinary description and expository expression. This is in effect due to the relationship that exists between spiritual traveling in Islām and the profound and blessed Word that *"Allāh is greater than that by which He can be described":*

اللَّهُ أَكْبَرُ مِنْ أَنْ يُوصَفَ.

For this reason, the earlier prophets themselves did not think of a station beyond that of witnessing Divine Names and Attributes so that they could set out on the wings of determination and fly toward that designated nest. Hence, whenever they were afflicted with various kinds of trials in the world, they would appeal to and find deliverance in the spiritual and supersensory initiatic power *(walāyat-i ma'nawī)* of the Noblest Messenger, Imām Amīr al-Mu'minīn 'Alī, al-Ṣādīqat al-Kubrā Fāṭimah Zahrā' and her pure offsprings. It was this very station of the Greatest Spiritual and Supersensory Initiatic authority *(walāyat-i kubrā-yi ma'nawīyah)* which delivered those prophets from their afflictions and ordeals.

Although undifferentiated characteristics of *wilāyah* were perceived *(mudrak)* by prophets of earlier times and on the basis of that they appealed to the exalted stations of the Pure Ones [Immaculate Imāms]; nonetheless, its qualities and specific details were unknown to them and remained so until the end of their lives. It is only from some verses of the Noble Qur'ān that one can find out that once or twice Abraham (peace be upon him) experienced a transient state—and not a perpetual station—that enabled him to witness higher realities and perfect Divine effusions. However, [as was mentioned before] that was a passing state and not a permanent station. The real nature and quality of *wilāyah,* in fact, will be actualized for him in the hereafter.

Before we refer to the verses of the Qur'ān to elaborate and explain this issue, we should mention that the station of sincerity possesses levels and gradations. According to the explicit injunction of the Qur'ān, some prophets did indeed attain the station of sincerity. Nevertheless, there is a more superior and more exalted station than that of sincerity, which they did not attain, and prayed and hoped to reach in the Hereafter. For instance, although according to the Qur'ānic ordinance, Joseph—may peace be upon him and upon our Prophet and his Family—was among those who were Sincere,

إِنَّهُ مِنْ عِبَادِنَا الْمُخْلَصِينَ.

Verily, he is one of Our sincere servants (12:24),

in his prayers he would beseech God to join him with the Righteous ones in their station, and he would supplicate saying:

أَنْتَ وَلِيِّي فِي الدُّنْيَا وَالآخِرَةِ تَوَفني مُسْلِماً وَأَلْحِقْنِي بِالصَّالِحِينَ.

> Thou art my Protecting Friend *(Walī)* in the world and the Hereafter, make me die a Muslim and join me to the Righteous ones. (12:10)

As is clear, he did not attain the station of righteousness in this world and prayed that this station may be granted to him after death and in the Hereafter. However, whether his prayers were answered and he attained the station of sincerity in the Hereafter cannot be inferred from the Qur'ānic verses. Similarly, though Abraham (peace be upon him) did possess a high rank in the station of sincerity, in his supplication he would say:

رَبِّ هَبْ لِي حُكْماً وَأَلْحِقْنِي بِالصَّالِحِينَ.

> My Lord, grant me wisdom and unite me with the Righteous. (26:83)

Hence, the status of the station of righteousness is higher than that of the station of sincerity; and Abraham begged his Lord to connect him to those who had attained this station. God did not fulfill his prayer in this world, but promised it to him in the Hereafter, saying:

وَلَقَدِ اصْطَفَيْنَاهُ فِي الدُّنيَا وَإِنَّهُ فِي الآخِرَةِ لَمِنَ الْصَّالِحِينَ.

> Verily we chose him in the world, and certainly in the Hereafter he is among the Righteous. (2:130)

It should be known that this level of righteousness which, according to the Qur'ān earlier prophets aspired to, is different from that which was granted to Abraham and his descendants, as we read in the statement of God, Exalted is He:

وَوَهَبْنَا لَهُ اسْحَاقَ وَيَعْقُوبَ نَافِلَةً وَكُلاًّ جَعَلْنَا صَالِحِينَ.

> And We bestowed upon him Isaac and Jacob as a gift,
> all of them We made Righteous. (21:72)

For all of them, including Abraham, possessed such an epithet. Nevertheless, Abraham prayed for the attainment of righteousness. Hence this station of righteousness is a more exalted and superior station.

The fact that the Prophet of Allāh (Muhammad) and some of his contemporaries had reached this same rank of righteousness is substantiated by the noble verse of the Qur'ān, which speaks on behalf of the Prophet himself:

إِنَّ وَلِيِّي اللَّهُ الَّذِي نَزَّلَ الْكِتَابَ وَهُوَ يَتَوَلَّى الصَّالِحِينَ.

> Verily, my Protecting Friend *(Walī)* is Allāh, Who has sent down the Scripture and He befriendeth the Righteous *(ṣāliḥīn)*. (7:196)

First of all, in this verse the Prophet affirms the absolute *walāyah* of the One over himself and says that, "my Protecting Friend *(Walī)* is He Who is the caretaker of the affairs of the righteous." Second, it becomes clear that at the time of the Prophet (peace be upon him) there lived some individuals from among the sincere ones who had reached the station of righteousness, and God, the Sustainer was the caretaker of their affairs. From what has been said, the mystery of the prayers of earlier prophets and their appeal to the Five Members of the Household of Purity *(Khamsah-yi*

Āl-i Ṭahārat), or to the Pure Imāms becomes clear; and the exalted status of the Imāms' station of righteousness becomes more evident; a status so exalted that Abraham beseeched God to be connected to them. That the great prophets of God had reached the station of sincerity can be inferred in several ways and spelled out in the noble verses of the Qur'ān.

First, through their praise *(ḥamd)* of God, as mentioned in the Glorious Qur'ān according to which no one but the sincere servants of God can invoke and praise the One as He deserves, God Almighty says:

سُبْحَانَ اللّٰهِ عَمَّا يَصِفُونَ إِلاَّ عِبَادَ اللّٰهِ الْمُخْلَصِينَ.

> Glorified is God from that which they attribute unto Him, except the sincere servants of Allāh. (37:160)

And God, the Exalted, commands His Prophet to praise Him, where He says:

قُلِ الْحَمْدُ لِلّٰهِ وَسَلاَمٌ عَلَى عِبَادِهِ الَّذِينَ اصْطَفَى اللّٰهُ خَيْرٌ أَمَّا يُشْرِكُونَ.

> Say (O Muhammad) praise belongs to God and Peace be upon His slaves whom He has chosen. Is God best, or what they ascribe as partners unto Him? (27:59)

And He describes the praise of Abraham may peace be upon him:

الْحَمْدُ لِلّٰهِ الَّذِي وَهَبَ لِي عَلَى الْكِبَرِ اسْمَاعِيلَ وَاسْحَاقَ إِنَّ رَبِّي لَسَمِيعُ الدُّعَاءِ.

> All Praise to Allāh, Who gave me Ishmael and Isaac in my old age, and surely my Lord *(rabbī)* is the Hearer of supplication. (14:39)

Or where God commands Noah, may Peace be upon him and our Prophet and his Family, to praise Him, saying:

فَقُلِ الْحَمْدُ لِلّهِ الَّذِي نَجَّانَا مِنَ الْقَوْمِ الظَّالِمِينَ

> Say: All Praise be to God, who hath saved us from the wrongdoing people. (23:28)

Second, there are explicit statements in the Noble Qur'ān concerning the station of sincerity that some of the great prophets attained. For example, concerning Joseph He says:

إِنَّهُ مِنْ عِبَادِنَا الْمُخْلَصِينَ.

> Verily he is among Our sincere servants. (12:24)

And concerning Moses He declares:

وَاذْكُرْ فِي الْكِتَابِ مُوسَى إِنَّهُ كَانَ مُخْلَصاً وَكَانَ رَسُولاً نَبِيّاً.

> And mention in the Book of Moses. Verily, he was sincere and a prophet and an apostle. (19:51)

And about Abraham, Isaac, and Jacob He states:

وَاذْكُرْ عِبَادَنَا ابْرَاهِيمَ وَاسْحَاقَ وَيَعْقُوبَ أُولِى الأَيْدِي وَالأَبْصَارِ

إِنَّا أَخْلَصْنَاهُمْ بِخَالِصَةٍ ذِكْرَى الدَّارِ.

> And mention also our servants Abraham and Isaac and Jacob, men of might and vision. Verily, We purified them with

> pure thought and with perpetual remembrance of the abode of the Hereafter. (38:45–46)

Third, through their benediction and gratitude toward God, Exalted is He. Because, on the one hand, in accordance with the noble verse of the Qur'ān, Satan has no access to the hearts of certain slaves of God who are among the sincere ones:

فَبِعِزَّتِكَ لأُغْوِيَنَّهُمْ أَجْمَعِينَ إِلاَّ عِبَادَكَ مِنْهُمُ الْمُخْلَصِينَ.

> By Your honor I will surely deceive them all, save thy servants who are among the sincere ones. (38:83)

And on the other hand, according to another noble verse, those servants of God deceived by Satan will not be among the grateful:

ثُمَّ لآتِيَنَّهُمْ مِنْ بَيْنِ أَيْدِيهِمْ وَمِنْ خَلْفِهِمْ وَعَنْ أَيْمَانِهِمْ وَعَنْ
شَمَائِلِهِمْ وَلاَ تَجِدُ أَكْثَرَهُمْ شَاكِرِينَ.

> Then I shall come upon them from before them and, from behind them, and from their right and left, and You will not find most of them grateful. (7:17)

Thus, we may conclude from these verses that the grateful, who are beyond the reach of Satan, are the same as the sincere servants. Therefore, if we come across people whom God, the Exalted, identifies in the Glorious Qur'ān with such traits as gratitude *(shukr)* and grateful *(shākir),* we understand that they are among the righteous ones. For example, one such person is Noah about whom God says:

ذُرِّيَّةَ مَنْ حَمَلْنَا مَعَ نُوحٍ إِنَّهُ كَانَ عَبْداً شَكُوراً.

(They were) the seed of those whom We carried with Noah (in the ark). Verily he was a grateful servant. (17:3)

And about the prophet Lot He says:

إِنَّا أَرْسَلْنَا عَلَيْهِمْ حَاصِباً إِلاَّ آلَ لُوطٍ نَجَّيْنَاهُمْ بِسَحَرٍ نِعْمَةً مِنْ عِنْدِنَا كَذَلِكَ نَجْزِي مَنْ شَكَرَ.

We sent a storm of stones upon them all, except the family of Lot, whom We rescued at dawn. As a grace from Us, thus We reward whoever gives thanks. (54:34–35)

And, finally, about Abraham God states:

إِنَّ ابْرَاهِيمَ كَانَ أُمَّةً قَانِتاً لِلَّهِ حَنِيفاً وَلَمْ يكُ مِنَ الْمُشْرِكِينَ شَاكِراً لأَنْعُمِهِ.

Indeed Abraham was a nation obedient to God, upright by nature *(ḥanīf)*, and he was not of the idolators; [he was] thankful for His bounties. (16:120–121)

In short, other prophets who have been identified with the quality of gratitude have all been among the sincere ones.

Fourth, is the epithet the chosen one *(ijtibā')*, which God, the Almighty and Majestic, has used in the Glorious Qur'ān to identify some prophets where He says:

وَوَهَبْنَا لَهُ اسْحَاقَ وَيَعْقُوبَ كُلاًّ هَدَيْنَا وَنُوحاً هَدَيْنَا مِنْ قَبْلُ وَمِنْ ذُرِّيَّتِهِ دَاوُدَ وَسُلَيْمَانَ وَأَيُّوبَ وَيُوسُفَ وَمُوسَى وَهَارُونَ وَكَذَلِكَ نَجْزِي الْمُحْسِنِينَ وَزَكَرِيَّا وَيَحْيَى وَعِيسَى وَإِلْيَاسَ كُلٌّ مِنَ الصَّالِحِينَ

وَاسْمَاعِيلَ وَالْيَسَعَ وَيُونُسَ وَلُوطاً وَكُلاًّ فَضَّلْنَا عَلَى الْعَالَمِينَ وَمِنْ آ
بَائِهِمْ وَذُرِّيَّاتِهِمْ وَاخْوَانِهِمْ وَاجْتَبَيْنَاهُمْ وَهَدَيْنَاهُمْ إِلَى صِرَاطٍ
مُسْتَقِيمٍ.

> And We bestowed upon him Isaac and Jacob—each of them We guided; and Noah did We guide before; and of his seed (We guided) David and Solomon, Jacob and Joseph, Moses, and Aaron. Thus, We reward the good ones *(muḥsinīn)*. And Zachary and John, Jesus and Elias; each one of them was of the righteous ones. And Ishmael and Elisha, Jonah and Lot—each one We chose above all creatures; and of their fathers, and of their offsprings and of their brethren; and We chose them and We guided them unto the straight path. (6:84–87)

In contrast to previous arguments whereby only those prophets mentioned by name were among the sincere ones, we can conclude from this noble verse that the station of sincerity, in fact, belonged to all prophets, may Peace be upon them. Our conclusion is based upon two premises.

First is the epithet *ijtibā'*. The word *ijtibā'* means 'selecting' or 'choosing' something from among many things that are from the same category and resemble one another. For instance, if someone picks up an apple for himself from a crate full of apples, his action is called *ijtiba'*. As God says in the above-mentioned noble verse "And We selected them *("wa ijtabaynāhum")* it means that He chose them from among all His creation and human beings for Himself and set them apart in an exclusive station. Therefore, their judgment is different from that of all other mortals. They are persons who have been selected and set aside, and in the true sense of the word exist solely for God and enjoy His special grace. It is obvious that this selection by God was based on the very same trait of sincerity; for the sincere ones on their part are those who exist solely for God and have completely severed all their ties to other creatures and have attached themselves to His Sacred Precinct.

Second, the term *ijtibā'* in this noble verse is not exclusive to a certain category of individuals. Although after mentioning Noah and Abraham and sixteen other prophets and their forefathers, descendants and brothers, God says, "We have chosen them"; nonetheless, it is obvious that by *'brethren'* God meant those who belong to their fraternity in matters of spirituality and ethics and are their comrades and fellow travelers in the pursuit of Divine Knowledge. Therefore, the verse can be interpreted in a nondelimited, or rather, universal sense, and one can infer from it the station of sincerity of all prophets.

Notes

1. 'Allāmah Sayyid Mahdī ibn Sayyid Murtaḍā al-Ṭabāṭabā'ī al-Najafī known as Baḥr al-'Ulūm, *Risāla-yi Sayr wa Sulūk,* edited and commented upon by 'Allāmah Sayyid Muhammad Ḥusayn Ḥusayni Tihrānī, Mashhad: Iran, 1996/1417 A.H.
2. Marfū'ah Barqī, *Kitāb al-Maḥāsin,* 1:222, #135. This *ḥadīth* is quoted from Imām 'Alī ibn Abī Ṭālib by Imām Ja'afar Ṣādiq. See Muhammad ibn Ya'qūb al-Kulaynī, *Uṣūl-i Kāfī,* 2:45.
3. Translation is borrowed from Seyyed Hossein Nasr, *Sufi Essays* (2d. ed.) Albany: State University of New York Press, 1991.
4. The term *baghy* has been mentioned in the Qur'ān on several occasions. See, 4:107, 10:23, and 42:42.
5. The term *'sih ṭalāqah'* literally means one divorcing one's wife three times. There is a provision in Islamic divorce law whereby a man, out of frustration announces three times his decision to divorce his wife. The divorce will be permanent without the possibility of reunion of the parties involved. If the couple decides to reunite, they have to marry and divorce a third person before they can marry each other again. It has been reported that Bāyazīd Basṭāmī said that "Once I prayed to His Threshhold and asked 'how can I reach You *(kayf al-wuṣūl ilayka)*?" I heard a voice addressing me that 'divorce yourself three times and then invoke Our Name *(ṭalaq nafsaka thalātha thumma qul Allāh)*." See Farīd al-Dīn 'Aṭṭār, *Taḍkirat al-Awliyā',* 1: 149.
6. Kulaynī, *Uṣūl al-Kāfī,* 2:289. (ed. Ḥājj Sayyid Javād Muṣṭafawī, Tehran n.d.)
7. Ismā'īl ibn Zayd Sukūnī was a student and companion of Imām Ja'afar

Ṣādiq and collected traditions narrated from the Shīʿī Imāms. For information on his life and career see, Muhammad ibn Ḥasan al-Ṭūsī known as Shaykh al-Ṭayʾfah, *Ikhtiyār Maʿrifat al-Rijāl,* Masshad, 1970, p. 147.

8. This statement is attributed to Bāyazīd Basṭāmī (d. 260–874). "As I reached the station of nearness *(qurb)* [to God], they told me to *'wish something.'* I said I have no wish, but you whish on my behalf. Again they said *'wish something,'* and I said 'I only want you.' They answered *'as long as an iota of particle of Bāyazīd's existence exists, this is an impossible wish, say farewell to your self and come,'* See, Farīd al-Dīn 'Aṭṭār, *Tadhkirat al-awliyāʾ,* 2:149.
9. Sayyid Ḥasan Āqā Qāḍī was the father of Ḥājj Mīrzā 'Alī Āqā Qāḍī. Ḥājj Mīrzā 'Alī taught jurisprudence, theology, and Ḥadīth in Najaf.
10. It is only after a wayfarer says farewell to his *self* that he is addressed as the *"soul at peace, return to your Lord pleased, well-pleasing, enter among My servants, enter My Garden."* (Qurʾān, 89: 27–30.) Many commentators translate the part of this verse that says *"fadkhulī fī ʿibādī"* as "enter among my servants." Shīʿī commentators translate this verse as "enter into the heart of my special servants (i.e., Imāms) [so that] you would enter my paradise" *fadkhulī jannatī.*

4

Undifferentiated Description of the Path and Methods of Wayfaring Toward God

Now that the details of the twelve realms of the wayfaring are known, we must proceed to discuss the method and manner of [spiritual] journeying and wayfaring. Two kinds of exposition will be presented here. The first is an undifferentiated and brief discussion, while the second will be a differentiated examination of wayfaring and spiritual journey.

Undifferentiated Description of the Path

The first essential task before the wayfarer is to undertake an investigation into different religions and creeds, and in consideration with his ability, try to discover the station of Divine Unity and the reality of His guidance, even by way of conjecture and mere preference. After affirmation of Divine Unity on the basis of knowledge or even by way of speculation, he should depart from the state of disbelief and heresy *(kufr)* and enter the realms of the Lesser Submission *(islām-i aṣghar)* and the Lesser Faith *(īmān-i aṣghar)*. This undertaking is unanimously considered as the duty of every individual who reaches the age of adolescence *(mukallaf)* and becomes mature and responsible. After much effort and search, if such a person [the *mukallaf*] fails to find preference [in a particular religion] and reach some degree of certainty, he must make a firm determination and persist in lamentation, weeping, and humility, and should not hesitate to resort to beseeching *(ibtihāl)* and pleading *(taḍarruʿ)* until ultimately a path is opened for him as it was opened for the Prophet Ḥaḍrat Idrīs and his disciples; may Peace be upon him and upon our Prophet and his Progeny.

The objective of beseeching and pleading is to have the wayfarer realize his helplessness and weakness, and ask for [Divine] guidance with a sincere heart. Obviously, God, Exalted is He, would not ever abandon His desperate and helpless servant who is in search of the Truth and the Reality.

وَالَّذِينَ جَاهَدُوا فِينَا لَنَهْدِيَنَّهُمْ سُبُلَنَا.

And those who struggle in Us, We shall assuredly guide them to Our ways. (29:69)

I remember that during the time that I was in Najaf Ashraf under the moral and spiritual guidance of the late Ḥājj Mīrzā ʿAlī Qāḍī, may God be pleased with him, one day at dawn while I was sitting on the prayer mat on the veranda, I fell asleep for a short time and had a vision. I dreamt of two men sitting in front of me. One of them was the Prophet Ḥaḍrat Idrīs—may peace be upon him and upon our Prophet and his Progeny—and the other was my dear and honorable brother Ḥājj Sayyid Muhammad Ḥasan Ṭabāṭabā'ī[1] who resides in Tabrīz at the present time. Ḥaḍrat Idrīs began a conversation with me in such a manner that he would converse and communicate his speech, but his utterances I heard from the tongue of my brother. Ḥaḍrat Idrīs said that "terrible events and accidents occurred in my life and resolving them seemed impossible to me by natural course of events and ordinary means. But they were all resolved unexpectedly. It became clear to me that a hand from the Invisible World and superior to ordinary means and causes was solving these problems and removing difficulties." This was the first transformation that connected the material world of nature to the supernatural realm for me. Our ties of connection [with Heaven] began from that point.

At that time it seemed to me that what Ḥaḍrat Idrīs meant by these tribulations were the hardships and afflictions of the days of his infancy and childhood. What I mean to emphasize is that if one pleads before his Sustainer in the matter of guidance with sincerity and truthfulness, He would certainly help and assist him. In those circumstances seeking the help of Qur'ānic verses that befit one's state would prove very useful and efficacious. God, Blessed and Exalted is He, has said:

آلَا بِذِكْرِ اللّٰهِ تَطْمَئِنُّ الْقُلُوبُ.

Lo! In the remembrance of God do hearts find certainty and serenity. (13:28)

Also invoking such Divine Names as:

يَا فَتَّاحُ، يَا دَلِيلَ الْمُتَحَيِّرِينَ.

O Opener! O Guide of the perplexed!

and the like, will prove to be effective. Of course, one must bear in mind that one must recite these prayers and verses with heart-felt sincerity and with utmost attention and presence.

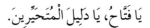

Once one of our friends related this story to us. He said, "Once I took a bus to go to Karbalā' and had the honor of making a pilgrimage to the shrine of Imām Ḥusayn, may God's greetings be upon him. My journey was from Iran. Next to my seat there sat a clean shaven and Westernized-looking young man. We did not engage in much conversation for some time. Suddenly, the young man began weeping. I was very surprised and asked him the reason for his crying. The young man said, 'If I do not trust to share [my story] with you, I can trust no one to share it with. I am a civil engineer. Since the time of my childhood years, I was raised in such a manner that I had no faith in religion. I was a materialist and did not believe in God or in creation and resurrection. But in my heart I felt strong love and affection for pious and religious people, whether they were Muslims, Christians, or Jews. One night I attended a party arranged by my friends, most of whom were of Bahāī' faith. For several hours we were busy dancing and having fun and so on. After some time I felt ashamed of myself and felt disgusted with my behavior. I left the room and went upstairs. There, alone, I cried for some time; a prayer arose from within me as if descending from Heaven: O God! You are the only God that there is! Help me! Then after a while I came downstairs. The night party came to an end, and we dispersed. The next day I set out for a technical assignment along with the railway chief and some senior officials. Suddenly, I saw a *Sayyid* (a descendant of the Prophet, peace be upon him) with a luminous face at a distance coming toward us. He approached me and greeted me. Then he said that he needs to see me and talk to me about a business. I promised to visit him the next day in the afternoon. Incidentally, after he left, one of my companions told me that the *Sayyid* was a saintly man and criticized me for returning his greeting so indifferently. I said it was because when the *Sayyid* greeted me, I thought that he was a begger and needed something and came to see me for that purpose. In the meantime, without advance notice, the railway chief ordered me to go to a certain place the next afternoon and assigned me to carry out a duty as he instructed, exactly at the same time that I had promised to meet the *Sayyid.* I concluded that I would not be able to visit the old man.

The next day when the time of my assignment was approaching, I began to feel sick. Gradually I was struck with such a high fever that I had to be hospitalized. They brought a physician to examine me. Naturally I had to excuse myself from the assignment given to me by the railway chief.

Soon afterward when the man who was sent to me by the railway chief had left, I realized that my fever subsided and my condition returned to normal. I found myself perfectly healthy once again. I concluded that there must be a mystery to this strange event. Therefore, I got up and went to the residence of that *Sayyid.* As soon as I sat down with him, he gave me an eloquent speech on the principal doctrine of the faith and with convincing reasons and proofs. His talk was so convincing that in no time he turned me into a believer. Then he gave me some instructions and asked me to return the next day. For several days I continued to meet him regularly. One day when I was in his presence, he described all the events of my day to me precisely as they had occurred. He also reflected in detail on all my acts and intentions that I never shared with anyone before and nobody was aware of except myself. At any rate, some time passed in this manner until one day I was compelled to attend a party with some friends. There, I was pushed to join them in gambling. The next day when I visited the *Sayyid* I found him furious. Without any introduction he turned to me and said that I must be terribly ashamed to have committed that mortal and capital sin again. I began to cry out of regret, admitted that my act was wrong, and promised to repent once and for all. He told me to go and make the Greater ablution, repent, and never commit that sin again. He also gave me some more instructions. In short, he changed the very course of my life. This incident occurred in Zanjān. Later, when I wanted to go to

Tehran he told me to go and visit certain *'ulamā* in Tehran. Finally, I was told to make a pilgrimage to the holy shrines of Karbalā' and Najaf. This is the journey that I am making at the behest of that *Sayyid.*'[2]

Our friend said: "In the vicinity of the border of Iraq, once again I noticed that the young man suddenly burst into tears. Again I asked him why he was crying. He told me that 'just as we entered the territory of Iraq, Ḥaḍrat Abā 'Abd Allāh al-Ḥusayn, may peace be upon him, welcomed me and extended his greeting to me.'"

My objective in narrating this episode is that if someone truly searches for God and the Truth with sincerity and pure intention, and seeks guidance from God wholeheartedly, he would certainly receive guidance even if he doubts the very existence of God.

At any rate, when the wayfarer succeeds at this stage, he should then set himself to find the Greater Submission *(islām-i akbar)* and the Greater Faith *(īmān-i akbar).* The first and most fundamental step at this point is to acquire the knowledge of the rules and injunctions of the *Sharī'ah,* which he must learn from a jurist *(faqīh).* When he has acquired such knowledge, he should put it into practice. In practice, too, he must be persistent until his certainty in and knowledge of God *(ma'rifat)* expands step by step. For knowledge is an heir to action, and action in turn is the inheritor of knowledge. If a person seriously has knowledge about and faith in something, he will, of necessity, try to make his actions conform to his knowledge and that which he perceives. The absence of action—in accordance with the law of cause and effect—indicates that one's knowledge is uncertain and his conviction is not total. Rather, the knowledge and faith he thought he possessed was merely reflection of illusion engraved in his ingenious faculty of imagination.

If one ever possesses true knowledge that the One God is the Absolute Sustainer and Provider, one should not exhaust his energy and endanger his life to accumulate wealth through every possible means. Rather, he should be content with making as much effort as has been enjoined by the *Sharī'ah,* and with utmost serenity and peace of mind, do his best to provide livelihood for his family and himself. But if one struggles excessively in search of livelihood or is overwhelmed by apprehension and anxiety, it is an indication that he knows God as a delimited rather than the Absolute Sustainer. He may believe that, for instance, God is the Provider only if he works hard and suffers hardships; as though God were his Provider only if He gave him money or monthly allowance, and so on.

Therefore, inward or outward anxiety is indicative of the lack of awareness that God is the Absolute Sustainer, or out of conviction that He is only a delimited Sustainer. In other words, this is an indication that one knows God to be a provider only under certain circumstances and conditions. This is what we mean when we say that action is the outcome of and heir to knowledge. An example that action is the result of knowledge is when one observes and admits his abasement before God when one recites:

سُبْحَانَ رَبِّيَ الأَعْلَى وَبِحَمْدِهِ.

Glory belongs to my Lord, Exalted is He, and Him do I praise.[3]

It is obvious that humility and lowliness cannot exist without exaltation. The humble will always stand in contrast to one who is exalted and majestic. Therefore, he will inevitably come to perceive the station of Absolute Majesty and then he will understand that Majesty is accompanied by knowledge and power. Hence, from a seemingly simple action, such as this prayer recited in prostration [in daily prayer], one becomes aware of the Absolute Majesty and the Absolute Power and Knowledge of God, Blessed and Exalted is He. This is the meaning of action being the product of knowledge. God Almighty refers to this fact in the following verse:

وَالْعَمَلُ الصَّالِحُ يَرْفَعُهُ.

And the pious deed does He Exalt. (35:10)

One must make utmost effort to observe obligatory duties and abstain from the forbidden *(muḥarramāt).* Because abandoning obligatory duties and committing the unlawful is in sharp conflict with traveling toward God. All the efforts of the traveler will be fruitful only when these two principles are observed together. Otherwise, in the same manner that golden adornment and ornaments are useless on a filthy body, so are the performance of supererogatory and ascetic acts prescribed by the *Sharī'ah* of no benefit for an impure heart and soul. Moreover, one must be conscientious to abstain from reprehensible acts *(makrūhāt)* and to fulfil the supererogatory ones, for attaining the stations of *islām-i akbar* and *īmān-i akbar* is contingent upon fulfilling these acts, because every act has a special property and efficacy which is peculiar to that particular act and leads one toward perfecting one's faith. The tradition narrated by Muhammad ibn Muslim points to this fact:

الايمَانُ لاَ يَكُونَ إلاَّ بِالْعَمَلِ، وَالْعَمَلُ مِنْهُ، وَلاَ يَثْبُتُ الايمَانُ إلاَّ بِالْعَمَلِ.

> Faith cannot be [actualized] without action, and action is a part of it. Faith will not be established except with action.

The spiritual traveler must therefore carry out every supererogatory act at least once so that he may benefit from its spiritual joy and efficacy. Hence it has been mentioned in the sermons of Amīr al-Mu'minīn 'Alī, may peace be upon him, that, "Perfect faith is the offspring of [perfect] action." Hence the traveler on the path of God must not be negligent of supererogatory acts in his journey toward the station of the Greater Faith *(īmān-i akbar)*. Obviously, his faith will remain imperfect to the same extent that he remains careless and negligent of performing these acts. For example, if a traveler purifies his tongue and all his bodily organs and makes them observant of the sacred manner and etiquette in the full sense of the term, but is not generous in spending his wealth [on the path of God], he would not advance beyond a certain stage and his faith would remain incomplete and imperfect. The very same imperfection would prevent his advancement to a higher station. Accordingly, he must have every bodily organ enjoy its share of faith until it achieves the degree of faith it deserves and is entitled to. For instance, the heart, which is the sovereign of the body, must be kept engaged in contemplation *(fikr)* and invocation *(dhikr)*. *Dhikr* means the heart's remembrance of the Names and Attributes of the Supreme Creator. Contemplation consists of deliberation and concentration of the heart on *"God's signs on the horizons and in their souls"*[4] and reflection over craftsmanship and scrutiny of the realm and process of creation. Through these acts, man's heart is nourished from the mainspring of faith:

آلاَ بِذِكْرِ اللّهِ تَطْمَئِنُّ القُلُوبُ.

> Lo! Verily in the remembrance of God do hearts find certainty and serenity. (13:28)

When every part of the traveler's corporeal being has received its share of the joy and efficacy of faith, he must begin spiritual combat *(mujāhadah)* whereby he can remove the imperfections of [his] *islām-i akbar* and *īmān-i akbar*, free himself from the bondage of doubt and speculation, and reach utmost certainty.

الَّذينَ آمَنُوا ولَمْ يَلْبِسُوا إيمَانَهُمْ بِظُلمٍ أُلَئِكَ لَهُمْ الأمْنُ وَهُمْ مُهْتَدُونَ.

> Those Who believe and do not vitiate their faith with wrongdoing, for them is safety and they are the rightly guided. (6:82)

The result of spiritual combat is that not only does it guide the wayfarer to the straight path, it also provides safety and immunity before the onslaught of Satans.

آلاَ إنَّ أوْلِيَاءَ اللّهِ لاَ خَوْفٌ عَلَيْهِمْ وَلاَ هُمْ يَحْزَنُونَ.

> Lo! Verily, friends of God are those on whom fear does not come, nor do they grieve. (10:62)

Fear *(khawf)* is being terrified by an occurrence that has not yet taken place, but is expected to take place sometime, and the thought of that causes agitation and anxiety. Grief *(ḥuzn)* is a feeling of sadness brought about by an undesirable and unpleasant event that has already taken place. These two states have no access to the heart of the traveler on God's path, for he has settled his matter with God once and for all, and has no objective and destination other than God. Neither will he grieve for an unawaited loss, nor shall he fear an unexpected event. This abode is the station of certainty *(yaqīn)* and God has called those who attain it His friends *(awliyā')*. The statement made by Amīr al-Mu'minīn 'Alī (may God's greetings be upon him) points to the station attained by such traveler :

أَبْصَرَ طَرِيقَهُ، وَسَلَكَ سَبِيلَهُ، وَعَرَفَ مَنَارَهُ، وَقَطَعَ غِمَارَهُ، فَهُوَ مِنَ الْيَقِينِ

عَلَى مِثْلِ ضَوْءِ الشَّمْسِ.

> . . . who has seen his way, has traversed his path, has recognized its minaret, and has removed its veils. He has attained a degree of certainty which is like the certainty of the rays of the sun.[5]

And in another statement he has described such a wayfarer in the following terms:

هَجَمَ بِهِمِ الْعِلْمُ عَلَى حَقِيقَةِ الْبَصِيرَةِ، وَبَاشَرُوا رُوحَ الْيَقِينِ،

وَاسْتَلاَنُوا مَا اسْتَوْعَرَهُ الْمُتْرَفُونَ، وَأَنِسُوا بِمَا اسْتَوْحَشَ مِنْهُ

هَجَمَ بِهِمِ الْعِلْمُ عَلَى حَقِيقَةِ الْبَصِيرَةِ، وَبَاشَرُوا رُوحَ الْيَقِينِ،

> The truth of the Knowledge of discernment descends upon them from all directions, and the spirit of certainty becomes their companion. That which seems harsh and difficult to the spoiled souls, becomes smooth and easy to them. They become intimate with what the ignorant is afraid of. They are confined in bodies in this world while their spirits dwell on the highest realms of the Kingdom [of God].[6]

It is at this stage that the gates of unveiling and vision *(kashf wa shuhūd)* shall be opened to the wayfarer.

It is obvious that traversing in this station is not in conflict with the traveler's [physical] presence in the world and his involvement in ordinary daily preoccupations. Inspirations descended upon his heart *(wāridāt-i qalbīyah)*[7] have no relevance to his outward conditions and preoccupations, such as marriage, profession, trade, farming, and the like. While he lives among the ordinary people and fulfills his worldly duties, his spirit travels in the realm of the Angelic Kingdom *(malakūt)* in the company of angels and heavenly beings. The example of such a traveler is like the example of a man who has been afflicted with a trauma, or has lost a beloved one. Although he lives amid the people, walks around, talks, eats, and sleeps like ordinary people, there is a storm in his heart that is caused by memories of his lost beloved, so much so, in fact, that whoever looks at him realizes that he is overwhelmed by sadness and grief.

While the traveler on the path of God is involved in normal activities, he has certain links and connections with God. Endless waves of yearning flow in his heart, and flames of love consume his inner being. The pain and suffering of separation melt his heart. No one except God is aware of his inner ferment. Yet, whoever looks at his countenance will realize that love of God, longing for the Truth, and quest for His Sacred Being has turned him into such a state.

This description makes it quite clear that lamentation, supplication, and invocation of the Immaculate [Shī'ite] Imāms, as reflected in the prayers narrated from them, were neither pretentious acts nor were they intended for teaching and guiding the people. Such misconceptions arise from ignorance and the lack of perception of realities on our part. Their stations are more exalted and their status much more noble than to let them make statements devoid of substance and truth, or to invite people toward God through a series of unpropitious supplications and meaningless prayers. Is it correct that we say that all those fiery and heart-warming invocations, weeping and lamentation of the Master of all masters, Ḥaḍrat Amīr al-Mu'minīn 'Alī, and those of Ḥaḍrat [Zayn al- 'Ābidīn] Sajjād, may God's greetings be upon them, were not genuine but were spurious and merely composed for educating others? Never! And by all means never! Those religious leaders and spiritual guides, may God's greetings be upon them all, had passed beyond the stages of wayfaring toward God, had entered into His sanctuary, and subsequently, had attained the station of subsistence after annihilation *(baqā' ba'd al-fanā')*, which is in fact, subsistence in the Beloved Worshiped One *(baqā' bil-ma'būd)*. Theirs are the states that contain the two realms of Unity and multiplicity *(waḥdat wa kathrat).* They see the light of Divine Unicity constantly in the manifestations of the world of contingency and in the multiplicity of God's Kingdom and Earth. Therefore, in accordance with the exalted degree of perfection they have achieved, they always observe the fundamentals of the realms of God's Kingdom and of the Earth. In other words, they do not withhold themselves from observing the most minute commands of the Divine Law, or manner, and/or any other conditions appropriate for their stations. At the same time, they keep their attention focused on the higher realms. That is the reason they are called the luminous creatures *(mawjūdāt-i nūrīyah).*

In any case, when the traveler successfully traverses these realms and overcomes Satan, he will enter the realm of triumph, whence it is time for him to proceed through the subsequent realms. By then the wayfarer has passed beyond the world of matter and entered the world of spirit where his greatest journey—that is, departure from the dominion of soul *(nafs)* and spirit *(rūḥ)* and transition from the abode of God's Kingdom to the abode of of Divine Majesty *(jabarūt)* and Divine Names *(lāhūt)*—will start.

Notes

1. ʿAllāmah Tihrānī reveals the identity of this Sayyid in another book as Āyatullāh Ḥājj Sayyid Maḥmūd Zanjānī, the Imām Jumʿah of Zanjān. See *Mihr-i Tābān,* p. 325.
2. Āyatullāh Ḥājj Sayyid Muhammad Ḥasan was the younger brother of ʿAllāmah Ṭabāṭabāʾī. Educated in Najaf, he taught philosophy and ethics in Tabrīz seminary until his death in 1967.
3. This formula is recited two times in each part *(rakʿah)* of the daily prayers when one's forehead touches the ground in prostration, each time followed by *Allāhū Akbar* (God is Great).
4. This is in reference to the Qurʾānic verse, *"And We shall show them our signs on the horizons and within themselves, until it will become clear to them that He Is the Truth."* (41:53)
5. ʿAlī ibn Abī Ṭālib, *Nahj al-Balāghah,* sermon #86, p. 210 (ed. with commentary by S. ʿAlīnaqī Fayḍ al-Islām), Tehran, 1365h/1944.
6. Ibid, sermon #139, pp. 1157–1158.
7. This term is in reference and allusion to Ṣadr al-Dīn Shīrāzī (Mullā

Ṣadrā) and his well-known work, *al-wāridāt al-qalbīyah fī maʿrifat al-rubūbīyah* (*The Inspirations of the Hearts Concerning Knowledge of the Divinity* [Tehran: Imperial Academy of Philosophy, 1978]).

The famous poem by Saʿadī of Shīrāz eloquently describes this state:

hargiz ḥadīth-i ḥāḍir-o ghāi'b shanīdehi'e?
man dar miyān-i jamʿ-o dilam jā-yi dīgar ast

Have you ever heard of the story of the one who is
present and absent at the same time?
I am in the middle of the crowd
and my heart is somewhere else.

5

Differentiated Description of the Path and Methods of Wayfaring Toward God

The method of wayfaring on the path of God consists of none other than invocation, contemplation, lamentation, and beseeching at the threshold of the Divine Throne who is, in fact, the only Fulfiller of our needs. This is possible only after one has made a covenant with and taken the oath of allegiance *(bay'ah)* to an enlightened spiritual master *(shaykh)* and a friend of God *(walī)*—one who has traversed beyond annihilation and reached the station of subsistence in God *(baqā'-i bi'llāh)*. The *shaykh* is a guide who is knowledgeable about that which is beneficial or harmful to the novice disciple in [the spiritual] life, and knows the means that lead to deliverance and salvation or damnation and perdition. He can take charge of the traveler's guidance and direct him toward the desired destination. However, one's journey through these stages is contingent upon several conditions that must be observed in the best possible and most perfect manner.

Abandoning Conventionalism, Habitual Practices, and Customs

The first step for the spiritual traveler to take is to abandon the contingent affairs *(umūr-i i'tibārīyah)*; those illusory and fictitious values, and conventional habits and practices that prevent him from traveling on the path. What we mean is that he should live in moderation among the people. Some people are constantly preoccupied with the rules and customs of society, and all their thoughts and efforts are centered on pleasing others and cultivating friendship. Such people are obsessed with formalities and welcome all kinds of interaction with various people, whether meaningful or useless, for the sake of maintaining their social status. They habitually subject themselves to these formalities in order to maintain their actual or imagined prestige, often exposing themselves to obligations and severe hardships. In order to preserve that which is peripheral, they set aside the very substance of life. They take common people's admiration and/or disapproval as criteria and waste their lives conforming to those standards. The vessel of their being is besieged with the tides of social habits and customs, swept hither and thither by the waves of social decorums and values of the society. Not knowing themselves, this group of people have no will power of their own, but are totally submissive to the will of society and follow that.

In sharp contrast to this group, there is another group of people who withdraw from society and people, renounce all kinds of social customs and norms, and free themselves from all societal obligations and privileges. They do not associate with or frequent the company of people, but live in their peaceful seclusion to the extent that their very seclusion brings them notoriety and recognition.

In order to attain his desired goal, the traveler must always observe moderation, adopt a middle position, refrain from either extreme, and walk on the straight path. This objective will not be achieved unless a reasonable degree of interaction is maintained with society. In such a situation, should a discord inevitably arise between the spiritual traveler and ordinary people as a result of the frequency and/or quality of their association, it would not be very harmful to the wayfarer. Of course, such a conflict will rarely arise because, while social intercourse is necessary and essential to a certain extent, the traveler would not under any circumstances submit himself [to follow] the manners and practices of the common people:

وَلاَ يَخَافُونَ [فِي اللّهِ] لَوْمَةَ لاَئِمٍ.

> And they do not fear the blame of any blamer [in matters relating to God]. (5:54)

This verse in effect points to the traveler's steadfastness in his pursuit of the straight path and his fortitude in his beliefs and practices. On the whole, one can say that the wayfarer must examine every social issue, evaluate its advantages and disadvantages, and never submit to the moral values and modalities of the masses of the people.

Steadfastness (ʿAzm)

When the traveler enters the arena of spiritual struggle, he will experience difficulties with and unpleasant behavior from ordinary people and acquaintances who are driven solely by their own whims and social ambitions. They blame him and disapprove of him with their words and deeds in order to dissuade him from his path and goal. They are particularly disturbed with the divergence and gap that appear between them and the wayfarer's lifestyle. They blame him and resort to various means to discourage the novice and stop him from pursuing the path. Of course, the traveler will encounter new problems at every stage of his journey that seem impossible to overcome without patience and determination. By resorting to the power and blessing of God, the traveler must have such strong will power that he can withstand all these difficulties, and with the weapons of patience and trust in God *(tawakkul)* annihilate them all. In consideration of the magnitude of his objective and goal, he should never be frightened by those terrible storms that are impediments and obstacles on his path toward God. In short, he should never let fear find its way into his heart, as the Holy Qurʾān says:

وَعَلَى اللّهِ فَلْيَتَوَكَّلِ الْمُؤْمِنُون

And in God let the believers put their trust. (3:160)

وَعَلَى اللّهِ فَلْيَتَوَكَّلِ الْمُتَوَكِّلُون.

And in God let the trusting put their trust. (14:12)

Compassion and Forbearance (Rifq wa Mudārā)

These are among the most important qualities that a traveler must cherish and possess. Not only will the slightest negligence in this regard hinder his advancement, it may even cause his permanent expulsion from wayfaring.

During the initial stages of his spiritual journey, the traveler may find an extraordinary degree of ferver and longing *(shoor va shawq)* in his heart, or may experience exceptional love and yearning when theophanies of Divine forms of Beauty *(tajallīyāt-i ṣūrīya-yi jamālīyah)* manifest themselves. As a result, he may resort to excessive prayer and invocation. He may spend a great deal of time in praying and wailing, doing every spiritual act and learning words from whoever he can and nurturing his soul with all kinds of spiritual nourishment. Not only is this kind of practice ineffective, it can also be harmful. Because as a result of imposing a heavy burden on his soul, the wayfarer's soul will react in a negative way and will hold back. Hence he will achieve no positive result and will eventually lose interest in performing even the most minor supererogatory prayers.

The mystery behind this exaggeration and the subsequent disappointment and withdrawal is that the wayfarer takes a temporary intellectual intuition and transient spiritual yearning as his criteria and motivation to perform those supererogatory rites and prayers, and places a heavy burden on the soul before preparing it. As soon as this transient longing disappears and the flame cools down, the soul feels exhausted and frustrated. Consequently, it drops the load and abandons the path in the beginning or the middle of the journey. It becomes alienated and develops an aversion to continue the journey and bear its numerous requirements and difficulties. Therefore, the traveler should never be deceived and misled by transient spiritual yearning. Quite the contrary, he should take into consideration his personal and professional condition, and realize his limitations and capacity with utmost care and foresight and undertake only what he can fulfil. To be sure, the traveler should even engage himself in acts somewhat lighter than his capacity but be persistent, so that he can fully benefit from the efficacies associated with them.

In consideration of this conclusion [we can say that] when the traveler is engaged in prayer, he should stop while he is still willing to continue so that a desire to and thirst for prayer always remains in his heart. The example of the traveler in relation to prayer is like that of a hungry man in relation to food. He must select the kind of food that would suit his taste and stop consuming food before he eats to his fill, so that the appetite and desire for food always remains with him. The advice that Ḥaḍrat Ṣādiq, may peace be upon him, gave to one of his disciples, a certain 'Abd al-'Azīz Qarāṭīsī, addresses this issue and emphasizes moderation in prayers:

يَا عَبْدَ الْعَزِيزِ إِنَّ لِلإِيمَانِ عَشْرَ دَرَجَاتٍ بِمَنْزِلَةِ السُّلَّمِ يُصْعَدُ مِنْهُ مِرْقَاةً بَعْدَ مِرْقَاتٍ إِلَى أَنْ قَالَ عليه السلام وَإِذَا رَأَيْتَ مَنْ هُوَ أَسْفَلُ مِنْكَ بِدَرَجَةٍ فَارْفَعْهُ إِلَيْكَ بِرِفْقٍ، وَلاَ تَحْمِلَنَّ عَلَيْهِ مَا لاَ يُطِيقُ فَتَكْسِرَهُ.

> O 'Abd al-'Azīz, verily there are ten levels for faith and it is like a ladder which must be climbed one step at a time. When you see someone who is a step lower than you are, lift him up gently to yourself, and do not impose a burden upon him which he cannot stand and that will break him.[1]

In short, from the forgoing discussion we can conclude that the most effective kind of prayer in the path of spiritual wayfaring and traveling is the one based on propensity and proclivity, as the statement of the Imām (Peace be upon him) indicates:

وَلاَ تُكْرِهُوا عَلَى أَنْفُسِكُمُ الْعِبَادَةَ.

> Do not impose worship upon your soul with reluctance.

Loyalty (Wafā')

Loyalty *(wafā)* consists of one's faithfulness to his repentance and abstinence from committing the same sin or wrongdoing once one repents. It is also fulfilling the commitments that he makes, and remaining loyal to the end to the covenant he makes with an enlightened spiritual guide and *shaykh* on the path of the Truth.

Stability and Perseverance (Thubāt wa Dawām)

Before we proceed to explain these concepts, a few introductory remarks are in order. What can be inferred from the Qur'ānic verses and sacred traditions indicate that the external entities perceived by our senses, or the acts we commit in the external world and are actualized in the material world, all contain truths that are beyond their external, material, and physical manifestations. In other words, beyond the outward and sensible realms there exist realities of a higher order that are independent of matter, time, space, and other accidents. When those realities descend from their actual states, in the external world they become corporialized in those material and sensible forms as we know them. The following verse of the Noble Qur'ān points to this question:

وَإِنْ مِنْ شَيْءٍ إِلاَّ عِنْدَنَا خَزَائِنُهُ وَمَا نُنَزِّلُهُ إِلاَّ بِقَدَرٍ مَعْلُومٍ.

> And there is not a thing but with Us, and We do not send it down except in an appointed measure. (15:21)

A brief interpretation of this verse tells us that, in general, everything has a different reality beyond measures and limitations prior to its actualization in the material world. However, with Knowledge and Will of the Supreme Creator, it is defined and confined in specific dimensions when it descends:

مَا أَصَابَ مِنْ مُصِيبَةٍ فِي الأَرْضِ وَلاَ فِي أَنْفُسِكُمْ إِلاَّ فِي كِتَابٍ مِنْ قَبْلِ

أَنْ نَبْرَأَهَا إِنَّ ذَلِكَ عَلَى اللَّهِ يَسِيرٌ.

> No affliction befalls the earth or in your souls, but it is in a book before We bring it into being. Verily that is easy for God. (57:22)

Since form in the manifested world is confined, limited, and subject to material accidents such as engendering, and corruption, it is, therefore, destined to decadence, deterioration, and perishing, as the Qur'ān says:

مَا عِنْدَكُمْ يَنْفَدُ.

> That which is with you will perish. (16:96)

However, those sublime and purified realities which are, in fact, Divine Treasures and whose nature is of the disengaged Angelic Kingdom are not subject to anything except, permanence, totality, and eternity, according to the Qur'ān:

وَمَا عِنْدَ اللَّهِ بَاقٍ.

> And that which is with God will remain. (16:96)

The following tradition, which is accepted unanimously by the Shī'ites and Sunnis alike refers to this reality:

نَحْنُ مَعَاشِرَ الأَنْبِيَاءِ أُمِرْنَا أَنْ نُكَلِّمَ النَّاسَ عَلَى قَدْرِ عُقُولِهِمْ.

> We the prophets have been commanded to speak to the people in accordance with the degree of their intellects.

This tradition addresses the qualitative, and not quantitative, aspects of revealing the truth. It indicates that God's prophets always brought the higher truths down to a lower cerebral plane appropriate to the intellectual capability and understanding of their audience, because human intellect is tainted by its attraction to illusive desires and worldly distractions, and cannot understand and appreciate or digest those truths in their original and pure states. Therefore, like a teacher who wants to describe the truth to simpleminded children in a manner compatible with their capacity to perceive the sensible things, the exalted prophets of God, by virtue of their status as protectors of the *Sharī'ah,* always brought those truths down to the level of human intellectual capacity and understanding. As promulgators and guardians of the *Sharī'ah,* the noble prophets sometimes explained those living truths in such a simple manner that gave the impression that they lack more profound meaning and sense. Whereas every external aspect and exoteric dimension of the *Sharī'ah,* such as daily prayers, fasting, pilgrimage to Mecca *(Ḥājj),* Holy War *(jihād),* payment of alms and charities, fulfillment of one's obligations toward one's kin, commanding the good and forbidding the reprehensible *(amr bil-maʿrūf wa nahy ʿan al-munkar),* all are living truths with profound intellectual, spiritual, and esoteric qualities and meanings.

The traveler is the one who, with God's help and blessing and in the course of wayfaring and spiritual combat, wants to remove all contaminations and impurities from his soul by resorting to humility, pleading, and beseeching; and with the help of pure intellect and enlightened soul, witness those exalted truths in this very darkened and material world. It is even possible that the wayfarer might witness the very simple rites of ablution and daily prayers in their actual celestial states and realize that they are thousands of times more exalted than their external corporeal and exoteric forms in terms of meaning and reflection. As we know, traditions narrated by the Immaculate Imāms, may God's peace and benediction be upon them, contain sublime and precious descriptions of the archetypal forms *(ṣuwar-i mithālī)* of rites of worship in the realm of the intermediate world and on the day of Resurrection when man [in effect] speaks to them. There is also a verse in the Glorious Qurʾān, according to which bodily organs possess the faculties of speech and hearing. Therefore, one must not think that, for example, a mosque is merely composed of mud and brick, but also has a living, intelligible, and perceptible reality. According to traditions, the Qurʾān and the mosque will complain [of man] before the Lord on the day of ressurrection.

It is reported that one day a traveler on the path of God was resting in his bed. As he wanted to turn from one side to the other, he suddenly heard the ground moan. When he searched for the cause, he perceived or was told that the ground was moaning because of separation from him![2]

Now that these preliminary remarks are made, we may say that, through perseverance in observing pertinent rites, the traveler must stabilize that pure angelic state in his soul so that he can transform his state into the station of second nature *(maqām-i malakah).* Through persistence in every single spiritual act, he must be able to derive utmost spiritual joy from that particular act and should not give up until he achieves this. The permanent angelic station of every spiritual act can be attained only when the traveler, steadily and persistently, is engaged in [performing] every spiritual act until the permanent effects of transient outward actions penetrate into the depth of his soul and are engraved in his soul in a manner that can no longer be removed.

Hence the traveler must try to choose only those spiritual acts and rites that are compatible with his capacity and chemistry; and if he is not determined to continue, he should not choose any act at all. Because when one abandons a spiritual act before completion, the [celestial] reality of that act will confront him and deprive him of its efficacy and positive effects. Consequently, there will emerge in the soul modes that are in conflict with the desired effects of that particular spiritual act. May God be our refuge [from such state].

The meaning of confrontation *(mukhāṣamah)* [in this context] is that when a traveler abandons a spiritual practice, in reaction the reality of that practice abandons him and takes away its efficacy and grace. Since a spiritual act is in essence good and luminous, when the soul is emptied of its effects, the void created in the soul of the wayfarer will be filled with darkness and evil. The fact is that "Nothing but good is found in God. As to the evil, ugliness, and darkness, they come solely from our own souls."

لَا يُوجَدُ عِندَ اللّهِ إِلَّا الْخَيْرُ وَأَمَّا الشُّرُورُ وَالْقَبَائِحُ وَالظُّلُمَاتُ إِنَّمَا هِيَ

مِنْ أَنْفُسِنَا.

Accordingly, every evil and ugliness that may arise is derived from our own souls and cannot be attributed to God.

وَالشَّرُّ لَيْسَ إِلَيْكَ.

And evil is not from You.

As this statement indicates it becomes clear that Divine emanations are not exclusive to certain people; rather, because of His kind Lordship and infinite mercy, they are extended to all human beings whether Muslims, Jews, Christians, or Zoroastrians, and even the worshipers of fire and idols. However, the qualities present in the recipients may lead them to make ill-advised choices. As a result His infinite mercy may produce delight, happiness and bliss in some people and anguish and grief in some others.

Constant Attention (Murāqabah)

Murāqabah means that the traveler must be attentive and alert under all circumstances so that he would not fail to observe his duties or stray from what he is assigned to do.

Murāqabah is a universal concept whose meaning varies according to difference in station, rank, and status of the traveler. At the early stages of wayfaring, *murāqabah* means avoiding the frivolous and abstaining from anything that is of no benefit either to one's religion or one's worldly life. It also means refraining from deeds and words that are in conflict with God's Will and His Pleasure. Gradually, however, *murāqabah* becomes more intense and exalted step by step. At times *murāqabah* aims only at one's concentration on one's silence; at other times on one's soul, and still at other times, on a higher plane; that is, on the reality of the Divine Names and Attributes. God willing, its details and stages will be explained in the coming pages.

It should be known that *murāqabah* is one of the most important requirements of spiritual traveling, and all prominent masters have placed considerable emphasis on it. Most of these masters consider *murāqabah* as one of the most important and necessary elements of wayfaring and traveling, for it is like the foundation stone upon which meditation *(fikr),* invocation *(dhikr)* and other requirements are constructed. Therefore, as long as *murāqabah* is not undertaken, meditation and invocation will remain ineffective. *Murāqabah* in relation to wayfaring, is like the necessity for a sick man to observe a healthy diet very strictly and refrain from inappropriate foods; whereas meditation and invocation are like medicines. As long as the sick person does not purify his body and refrain from consuming foods that do not suit his condition, medicine will remain ineffective, or may even produce adverse effects. Hence, prominent sages and masters of the path inhibit the wayfarer from meditation and invocation without *murāqabah,* and prescribe them only in consideration with the rank and station of the wayfarer.

Self-Accounting (Muḥāsabah)

Muḥāsabah consists of one's scrutiny of one's own actions. It requires assigning certain amount of time during the day and night to examine one's daily acts and deeds. Ḥaḍrat Mūsā ibn Ja'far [the seventh Imām] may peace be upon him, pointed to this undertaking in the following statement:

لَيْسَ مِنَّا مَنْ لَمْ يُحَاسِبْ نَفْسَهُ كُلَّ يَوْمٍ مَرَّةً.

> He who does not scrutinize the account of his own soul once every day is not one of us.[3]

In the course of self-scrutiny, if the traveler realizes that he has violated his duties, he must resort to *istighfār,* that is to say, ask God for forgiveness. Otherwise, he must express his gratitude to God, the Exalted for enabling him to perform his duties [toward God].

Self-Condemnation (Mu'ākhadhah)

When the traveler realizes that his carnal soul betrays him, he should set himself to discipline his soul and direct it in any manner he sees appropriate.

Expeditious Action (Musāra'at)

Musāra'at (Arabic *musāra'ah*) means that the wayfarer must take immediate and expeditious action to carry out whatever he decides [in the process of and in relation to wayfaring]. Because there are many calamities and tribulations on this path and many obstacles may emerge on the traveler's path in accordance with his station, he must be very alert and judicious, and carry out his duties before an obstacle emerges on his way and preoccupies him. He must not leave any stone unturned in achieving his objectives and reaching his destination.

Devotion (Irādat)

Irādat means devotion and love for the Master of religion *(ṣāḥib al-Sharī'ah)* [i.e., the Prophet] and his legitimate successors [the Imāms]. The wayfarer must be sincere and pure in his devotion to the extent that no doubt would remain [in his heart]. He must achieve utmost perfection in this station. Because devotion plays a major part in the effectiveness and impact of spiritual practices upon the soul. The more sincere and intense the devotion, the deeper and firmer the impact of rituals will be upon the wayfarer's soul.

Since all existents are God's creatures, the traveler must love them all and respect them in accordance with their ranks and status. Compassion and kindness toward God's creatures in accordance with their station and rank, whether human beings or animals, is indeed a sign of love for God. As it has been stated in traditions, the most important aspect of faith is love and compassion toward God's creation.

إلَهِي أسْألُكَ حُبَّكَ وَحُبَّ مَنْ يُحِبُّكَ

O my God, I beseech You to grant me Your love and the love of those who love You.

أُحِبُّ بِحُبِّهَا تَلَعَاتِ نَجْدٍ وَمَا شَغَفِي بِهَا لَوْلاَ هَوَاهَا

أذِلُّ لآلِ لَيْلَى فِي هَوَاهَا وَأحْتَمِلُ الأصَاغِرَ وَالْكِبَارَا

Because of loving her, I love the sand dues of Najd
And I would not be infatuated with them, if not for her longing.
In longing for Layla, I humble myself to her folks,
And bear the humble and the noble among them.[4]

Proper Manner (Adab)

Adab means proper manner and reverence before God, the Lord of Majesty and His vicegerents. It is different from the love and devotion mentioned above. For reverence means being careful of and attentive to one's behavior and acts lest one trespass one's limits and commit acts contrary to the essentials of servanthood. That is because there are limits and bounds for the contingent being in relation to the Necessary Being. The necessity of keeping proper manner [in relation to God] is observing the requirements of the world of multiplicity. Whereas love and devotion is an attraction toward the Sacred Precinct and necessitates attention to and focus on Divine Unity.

The relation between *irādat* and *adab* is like the relationship that exists between obligatory rites *(wājib)* and the forbidden ones *(ḥarām)* in the *Sharī'ah;* for in fulfilling the obligatory rites, the traveler's attention is focused on the Beloved, whereas in refraining from the *ḥarām* he concentrates on his own boundaries lest he trespass the bounds of contingency and violate the requirements of servanthood. In fact, observing *adab* is like taking a middle ground between fear and hope *(khawf wa rajā'),* and the outcome of its absence is immensity of expansion *(inbisāṭ),* which would not be desirable if it exceeds a reasonable extent.

The late Ḥājj Mīrzā 'Alī Qāḍī, may God be pleased with him, was in a station in which expansion and devotion dominated over his fear. The state of the late Ḥājj Shaykh Muhammad Bahārī, may God's mercy be upon him, was also similar to this. In contrast, in the case of Ḥājj Mīrzā Javād Āqā Malikī Tabrīzī, may God be pleased with him, the station of fear dominated over that of hope and expansion, as can be understood from allusions and hints in his discourses.[5] The one [in whose soul] the station of expansion is dominant is called *kharābātī* (lit.) "tavern haunter"; and one whose fear is greater is named *munājātī* (supplicator). But perfection lies in the observance of moderation, and that consists of possessing utmost expansion along with utmost fear. This station is enjoyed exclusively by the Immaculate Imāms, may God's benediction and peace be upon them all.

Let us now return to the main point of our discussion. We can conclude that proper manner requires that the contingent being never forgets his boundaries and limitations of contingency. That is why whenever one made a statement in the presence of Ḥaḍrat Ṣādiq—may God's greetings be upon him—that had a slight nature of exaggeration *(ghuluw),* he would immediately throw himself down in a posture of adoration, submission, and prostration.

The perfect degree of *adab* is that in all conditions and under all circumstances the traveler must see himself in the presence of God, the Glorious and the Exalted, and observe the rules of etiquette in his speech and silence, in eating and sleeping, while moving about or resting, and in short, in all states and conditions, movements and pauses. If the traveler's attention is constantly focused on the Names and Attributes of God, proper manner and humility will inevitably become evident in him.

Intention (Niyyat)

Niyyat (Arabic *Niyyah*) means that the traveler should not have any other objective in his spiritual journey except mere wayfaring and annihilation in the Divine Essence. Therefore, the traveler's quest must be sincere and pure:

فَادْعُوا اللَّهَ مُخْلِصِينَ لَهُ الدِّينَ.

> So [O believer] pray unto Allāh purifying religion for Him. (40:14)

It is mentioned in many traditions that intention has three levels. According to one tradition attributed to Imām Ṣādiq, may God's greetings be upon him:

العُبَّادُ ثَلاَثَةٌ: قَوْمٌ عَبَدُوا اللَّهَ خَوْفاً فَتِلْكَ عِبَادَةُ الْعَبِيدِ، وَقَوْمٌ عَبَدُوا اللَّهَ طَمْعاً فَتِلْكَ عِبَادَةُ الأجرَاءِ، وَقَوْمٌ عَبَدُوا اللَّهَ حُبّاً فَتِلْكَ عِبَادَةُ الأحْرَارِ.

> Worshipers are of three categories: Those who worship God out of fear; that is the worship of slaves and bondsmen. Those who worship Him out of greed; that is the worship of merchants. And finally, those who worship Him out of love; and this is the worship of free-spirited men [i.e., gnostics *('urafā')*].

If one can contemplate and meditate on this statement, one will realize that the worship of the first two groups of people is not—in effect—correct because they do not worship God for the sake of God. Rather, they are motivated by self-interest and self-love. In fact, they worship themselves, not God, Exalted is He, because their point of reference and the motives behind their worship are self-interest and appetites of the carnal soul. Since self-worship is not congruent with worshiping God according to the first argument, this group of people deny God and are therefore not true believers. But the Noble Qur'ān explicitly describes the worshiping God as primordial human state and rejects any kind of change and alteration in creation:

فَأَقِمْ وَجْهَكَ لِلدِّينِ حَنِيفاً فِطْرَةَ اللَّهِ الَّتِي فَطَرَ النَّاسَ عَلَيْهَا لاَ
تَبْدِيلَ لِخَلْقِ اللَّهِ ذَلِكَ الدِّينُ الْقَيِّمُ وَلَكِنَّ أَكْثَرَ النَّاسِ لاَ يَعْلَمُونَ.

> So set your purpose for religion as a primordial believer upright by nature, the innate nature of Allāh in which He has created man. There is no altering in God's creation. That is the right religion, but most people do not know. (30:30)

Accordingly, man's deviation is not from the path of worshiping God, but from the path of Divine Unity. As a result, man does not see unity in God's acts and attributes, but assigns partners to Him. That is the reason the Holy Qur'ān frequently affirms the Unity of God and rejects partnership in relation to Him. On this basis, the first two groups regard God as an associate and a partner in their own personal objectives; while they worship God, they do not stop worshiping themselves. They carry out their acts of worship with two objectives in mind, and this is mere polytheism *(shirk)*. In fact, these two groups are polytheist *(mushrikīn)* in relation to God, Exalted is He, which according to the explicit text of the Qur'ān is an unforgivable act:

إِنَّ اللَّهَ لاَ يَغْفِرُ أَنْ يُشْرَكَ بِهِ وَيَغْفِرُ مَا دُونَ ذَلِكَ لِمَنْ يَشَاءُ.

> Verily, God does not forgive that a partner should be ascribed to Him, other than that He forgives whom He wills. (4:47)

Accordingly, the worship of this group of people will never be fruitful, nor will it bring them closer to God, Exalted is He.

As to the third group of people who worship God out of love for Him, theirs is the worship of free-spirited men as is emphasized in many traditions:

تِلْكَ عِبَادَةُ الْكِرَامِ.

That is the worship of the noble ones.

This is the genuine and proper kind of worship, which is not attainable by everyone, except the pure ones of the Divine Threshold:

فَهٰذَا مَقَامٌ مَكْنُونٌ لاَ يَمَسُّهُ إلاَّ الْمُطَهَّرُونَ.

This is the hidden station, untouched by anyone except the pure ones.

Love is defined as an attraction, that is, one's being pulled in a direction or toward a truth. The third group of worshipers are those who base their worship [of God] on the foundation of love and attraction toward Him. They have no objective in mind except being drawn toward God and finding proximity to Him. Only the mere attraction that they feel in their hearts toward the Beloved is the motive that drives them toward the Beloved and is the cause of their journey toward His sacred sanctuary.

It is mentioned in some traditions that we should worship God, the Exalted, because He is worthy of worship. It is obvious that God's worthiness to be worshiped does not emanate from His Attributes but from His Divine Essence, glorious is His Majesty and great is His State. In short, it means that we must worship God because He is God.

إلٰهي مَا عَبَدْتُكَ خَوْفاً مِنْ نَارِكَ وَلاَ طَمَعاً فِي جَنَّتِكَ، بَلْ وَجَدْتُكَ

أهْلاً لِلْعِبَادَةِ فَعَبَدْتُكَ.

أنْتَ دَلَلْتَنِي عَلَيْكَ، وَدَعَوْتَنِي إلَيْكَ، وَلَوْلاَ أنْتَ لَمْ أدْرِ مَا أنْتَ.

> O my Lord, I did not worship Thee out of fear of the fire of Your hell, nor for the greed of Your paradise. But because I found only Thee worthy of worship, so I worshiped Thee. You have guided me unto Yourself and have called me to Thyself, and were it not for Thee I could never have known Thee as Thee art.

The traveler on the path of God begins the first step of his journey with love. However, after traversing certain stations and attaining some degree of perfection, he feels that love and the Beloved are two distinct and separate entities. Therefore, he tries to set aside love that had thus far been a necessary provision for his journey and spiritual advancement toward God. He realizes that love, which was an effective means up to this point, is becoming harmful and an obstacle to his advancement on the path. As a result, from then on the traveler has only the Beloved in mind and only worships Him as the sole Beloved.

Still, when the traveler advances further on the path and passes some other stations, he understands that even this kind of worship is not free from the tarnish of polytheism, for in this type of worship he sees himself as the lover and God as the Beloved. Being conscious of one's selfhood and seeing the lover independent of the Beloved implies *otherness* and *duality* and is in contradiction with loving the Beloved. Therefore, having the Beloved in mind while one carries the title of lover is in contradiction with worshiping the Sacred Essence of God. Consequently, from this point on the traveler tries to discount love and the beloved as two so that he can overcome *otherness* and pass beyond the realm of multiplicity and enter the world of Unity. At this time even intention *(niyyat)* disappears from the heart of the wayfarer because there is no longer a personal identity and selfhood from which intention would originate.

Until the beginning of this station, the traveler had sought Gnostic vision *(shuhūd),* unveiling *(kashf),* and disclosure *(mukāshafah).* At this point he becomes oblivious to them all, for he no longer possesses independent will to have any goal or objective in mind other than the Beloved. The wayfarer's eyes and heart renounce the presence and/or absence of visions, reaching or not reaching the goal, knowledge or ignorance, and acceptance or rejection. As Ḥāfiẓ of Shīrāz says:

با خرابات نشینان زکرامات ملاف

هرسخن جائی وهرنکته مقامی دارد

Do not brag of miraculous wonders before the tavern haunters,
Every saying fits a certain occasion and each point a proper place.

It is related that Bāyazīd Basṭāmī once said, "I renounced the world on the first day, and the Hereafter on the second; the third day I renounced everything other than God, and on the fourth I was asked,

مَا تُرِيدُ ؟

"What do you want?" and I said:

أُرِيدُ أَنْ لاَ أُرِيدَ.

"I want not to want!"[6]

The above quotation alludes to the fourfold stations that have been discussed by some sages. The first station is the renunciation of the world; the second is the renunciation of the Hereafter, the third is the renunciation of the Master *(mawlā);* and the fourth is the renunciation of renunciation. Reflect deeply upon this statement.

Among the spiritual travelers the term "renunciation of greed" *(qaṭ'-i ṭama')* alludes to this station, which is a very important and arduous stage, and like a rugged valley, passing through it is a formidable task. For after so much soul-searching and self-questioning, the traveler finds out that in all stages of his wayfaring he was never free of personal intention and objective. On the contrary, he always carried certain ambitions and expectations in the depth of his heart, even though those ambitions might have been about overcoming weaknesses and imperfections from his soul and attaining spiritual excellence and perfection. If the traveler struggles to disengage his mind and thought, and forces himself to go through this narrow passage and free and detach himself from those objectives and goals, he will achieve no results. Because the very same struggle to attain detachment and catharsis *(tajrīd)* implies the presence of attachment and is an indication of the wayfarer's struggle for a special [personal] purpose. The existence of this purpose by itself is a sign of the absence of detachment of the soul.

One day I discussed this mystery with my teacher and mentor, the late Āqā Ḥājj Mīrzā ʿAlī Āqā Qāḍī, may God be pleased with him, and pleaded for [his help] to find a solution. He said: "This problem can be solved by resorting to purification through incineration *(iḥrāq)*. The traveler must understand and accept the fact that God, Exalted is He, has created him a covetous being. No matter how much he struggles to overcome his greed, he will not succeed, for greed is part of his innate nature. A desire to eliminate greed from the soul implies the presence of a greed of a higher nature for which he abandoned the lower one. Therefore, when he finds himself helpless and unable to free himself of greed, he will have to entrust his affair to God and set aside any thought of eradicating greed from his soul by himself. The admission of helplessness and weakness burns down the very root of greed and purifies him."

One should realize, of course, that experiencing this state is not possible through discursive speculation. Rather, true understanding of this notion requires experiencing a special state and intellectual intuition *(dhawq)*. If one can experience this state through intellectual intuition once in life, one would realize that all pleasures of the world could not match the joy of experiencing this truth.

The reason for calling this method incineration is that it destroys and burns down the very roots of one's identities, intentions, anxieties, and problems, and does not let an iota of their trace remain in the traveler's being.

There are references to *iḥrāq* in the Noble Qur'ān on several occasions. If one uses this method to attain the goal and move on the path, in a short time one can traverse stations that would otherwise take several years to pass. One of the cases of reference to *iḥrāq* in the Glorious Qur'ān is the utterance of rememberance of return to God *(istirjāʿ)*:

إِنَّا لِلَّهِ وَإِنَّا إِلَيْهِ رَاجِعُونَ.

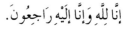

Verily we belong to God and unto Him we shall return. (2:156)

At times of adversity, difficulties, and affliction, man can console himself in several ways. For instance, he may remind himself that every man is bound to experience misfortune or die; and in doing so, he can gradually comfort himself. By means of *iḥrāqīyah* and *istirjāʿ*, however, God shortens the way and solves the problem once and for all. For if man reminds himself that his existence and whatever he possesses belong to God who granted them to him when He willed and will take them away whenever He wills and no one else has any authority to interfere; if man realizes that he, in fact, did not own anything from the beginning and his ownership of his wealth was metaphorical, he would not be distressed and saddened by its loss. This realization will pave the way for him and will comfort his soul and help him to bear his loss and deprivation.

Realizing that God created man covetous from the beginning is like perceiving that God, the nondelimited Possessor of wealth *(ghanī-ye alā'l iṭlāq),* created His servant poor from the very beginning, and placed poverty in his nature. Therefore, there is no need for reason to prove man's inherent poverty and his need to beg, which poverty necessitates. One cannot blame the begger when he begs, because poverty calls for begging. Therefore, if the wayfarer on the path of God realizes his greed, he must understand that God has created his being with this attribute and under no circumstances can he free himself from it. On the other hand, since annihilation in the Divine Essence, which is founded on the basis of the prayer of the free-spirited men *(aḥrār)* [sing. *ḥurr*], is not in harmony with covetousness, the wayfarer feels totally helpless and anguished. Ironically, this very same feeling helps him go beyond the boundaries of his *selfhood,* which is accompanied by greed. After passing through this stage there is no longer I-*ness (ennīyat)* and *selfhood* left to associate with greed and desire. [It is important] that one contemplates this point and understands it properly.

Silence (Ṣamt)

There are two categories of silence: (1) silence in general is called *muḍāf,* and (2) absolute and particular silence is known as *muṭlaq*. General silence is to withhold the tongue from superfluous speech with ordinary people.

In other words, the traveler must limit his conversation as much as possible to what is absolutely necessary. General silence is essential and even commendable at all times throughout the course of wayfaring. The statement of the Imām, may God's greetings be upon him, refers to this silence:

إنَّ شِيعَتَنَا الْخُرْسُ.

> Surely, our followers are the mute ones.[7]

Also the tradition attributed to Ḥaḍrat Ṣādiq may peace be upon him in the *Miṣbāḥ al-Sharīʿah* alludes to silence in general:

الصَّمْتُ شِعَارُ الْمُحِبِّينَ، وَفِيهِ رِضَا الرَّبِّ، وَهُوَ مِنْ أَخْلاَقِ الأَنْبِيَاءِ وَشِعَارِ الأَصْفِيَاءِ.

> Silence is the motto of the lovers [of God], and in it lies the Lord's pleasure. It is the virtue of the prophets and the motto of the pure ones.[8]

In the tradition attributed to Ḥaḍrat Riḍā (peace be upon him) and narrated by Baznaṭī, it is mentioned that:

الصَّمْتُ بَابٌ مِنْ أَبْوَابِ الْحِكْمَةِ، وَإِنَّهُ دَلِيلٌ عَلَى كُلِّ خَيْرٍ.

> Silence is a gate from among the gates of wisdom, and it is indeed the guide to every good.[9]

The second is the absolute and particular silence and is defined as withholding the tongue from conversation with all people while one is engaged in invocations *(adhkār),* whose number, timing, and length are prescribed [by the *shaykh*]. Otherwise, it is not commendable to observe absolute silence in other situations.

Abstaining from Indulgence in Food Consumption (Jaūʿ)

Jaūʿ or abstaining from indulgence in food consumption is permissible and recommended to the extent that it would not lead to starvation and weakness or alteration of one's mental state. Imām Ṣādiq may peace be upon him said:

الْجُوعُ إِدَامُ الْمُؤْمِنِ، وَغِذَاءُ الرُّوحِ، وَطَعَامُ الْقَلْبِ.

Hunger is the believer's condiment, the spirit's nourishment, and the heart's food.[10]

Abstaining from indulgence in food consumption results in purification and illumination of the soul, and imaginal power and thought can fly high in hunger. Indulgence in food consumption, in contrast, results in exhaustion and heaviness of the soul and prevents it from flying high in the sky of gnosis. Fasting is one of the most commendable rites of worship. There are fascinating descriptions of fasting and its effects in wayfaring and spiritual journey in the account of the Prophet's nocturnal ascent *(miʿrāj).* It is described in detail in [Abū al-Ḥasan Muhammad] Daylamī's book, *Irshād al-qulūb* and volume seventeen of [Muhammad Bāqir] Majlisī's *Biḥār al-anwār,* wherein God addresses His beloved Messenger (Peace be upon him) with the title of *O! Aḥmad*—the Praised One.[11] Our master and teacher, the late Āyatullāh Qāḍī, may God be pleased with him, once related a fascinating story on the issue of fasting and hunger.

"It has been said that during the time of the earlier prophets there were three friends [traveling] who entered a town where they were strangers. At nightfall they dispersed in different directions to provide food for themselves. They decided to meet each other at the same place and at a certain time the next day. One of them received an invitation and the other invited himself to someone's home. The third one who had no place to go said to himself, 'I will go to the mosque and be God's guest.' He went to the mosque where he stayed overnight but remained hungry until the next morning. The next day the three men met at the designated place and began to describe what had befallen them. A revelation from God, Exalted is He, came to His prophet of the time whereby He ordered him to 'Tell the guest of Ours that We accepted to host this dear guest. We desired to offer him the best of foods, but We searched Our Invisible Treasures and did not find any food for him better than fasting and hunger.'"

Spiritual Retreat (Khalwat)

Like silence, spiritual retreat *(khalwat,* Arabic *khalwah)* is also of two categories: general and particular.

General spiritual retreat *(khalwat-i 'ām)* consists of seclusion and withdrawal from association with profane people and those who are not people of God *(ahl Allāh),* and in particular [maintaining] as little conjunction as needed with the weak-minded among the common people.

وَذَرِ الَّذِينَ اتَّخَذُوا دِينَهُمْ لَعِباً وَلَهْواً وَغَرَّتْهُمُ الْحَيَوةُ الدُّنْيَا.

> And forsake those who take their religion for a pastime and a jest, and whom the life of the world deceives. (6:70)

As to the particular spiritual retreat *(khalwat-i khāṣṣ),* it is distancing oneself from all people. Although particular retreat is spiritually beneficial at all times and during all kinds of prayer and invocation, it is especially required during certain types of verbal invocations *(adhkār-i kalāmīyah)* and possibly in all of them, and is considered essential by the masters of the path. There are several prerequisites that must be observed in this regard. These include withdrawal from the crowd and noisy places and avoidance from hearing any kind of disturbing voice and sound. In addition, the place of particular retreat must be legally sanctioned by the *Sharī'ah* to use for that purpose, and must be of ritual purity *(ṭahārah)* from the walls to the roof. It should also be large enough to room only one person; and must have nothing of worldly embellishments in it, because the small size of the prayer room and the absence of furnishings in it contributes to one's concentration and serenity.

A man asked Salmān Fārsī[12] may God be pleased with him, for permission to build a house for him, as he had not built a house for himself until that time. Salmān would not permit him to do so. The man said, "I know the reason you do not permit me." Salmān said, "Tell me what could the reason be?" The man replied, "The reason is that you would like me to build a house whose length and width are about the size of your body, and such a house is not feasible to build." Salmān said, "Yes, you are right." Then that man received the permission to build such a house for him, and he built it.

Morning Wakefulness (Sahar)

Sahar means being awake at dawn to the extent permitted by the traveler's constitution. About the reprehensibility of sleeping at daybreak and the praiseworthiness of being awake during that time, God, the Exalted says:

كَانُوا قَلِيلاً مِنَ اللَّيْلِ مَا يَهْجَعُونَ وَبِالأَسْحَارِ هُمْ يَسْتَغْفِرُونَ.

> Little of the night they would slumber, and at dawn they would seek forgiveness. (6:70)

Constant Observance of Ritual Cleanliness (Ṭahārah)

Ritual cleanliness *(ṭahārat,* Arabic *ṭahārah)* is being in the state of the Lesser ablution *(wuḍū')* at all times, and performing the obligatory Greater ablutions *(aghsāl-i wājibah)* (sing. *ghusl*), and the Greater ablution on Fridays and other supererogatory *(mustaḥabb)* ablutions to the extent possible.

Extreme Humility (Taḍarruʿ)

Taḍarruʿ means constant expression of humility to the point of exaggeration and one's recognition of one's nothingness at all times, and resorting to lamentation [before God].

Curbing Desires for Worldly Pleasures

This virtue includes refraining from pleasures and appetites to the extent that one's capacity and constitution permits, and confining oneself to what is necessary for maintenance of one's health and subsistence.

Guarding the Mysteries [of the Path] (Kitmān-i sirr)

This virtue is one of the most important conditions of spiritual journeying. Prominent sages devoted much effort to it and strongly recommended that their disciples observe this principle. They insisted upon it to the point of exaggeration whether in practical matters related to prayers, litanies, and formulae for invocation *(awrād wa adhkār)*, or in matters related to inspirations, spiritual states, and disclosures. Even on occasions when expedient dissimulation *(taqīyah)*[13] is impossible and the disclosure of secrets becomes unavoidable or imperative, they have regarded keeping the secrets of the path as part of the essential elements and binding instructions. Even if concealing the secrets of the path calls for abandoning a ritual or a prayer, the traveler must comply with that.

وَاسْتَعِينُوا عَلَى حَوَائِجِكُمْ بِالْكِتْمَانِ.

> Seek help concerning your needs through concealment and secrecy.

By resorting to expedient dissimulation *(taqīyah)* and secrecy, many ordeals and difficulties can be reduced or even avoided; whereas disregarding it can cause the traveler to face many tribulations and afflictions. In any case, when difficulties do arise one must advance on the path with patience and forbearance so that one can become triumphant.

وَاسْتَعِينُوا بِالصَّبْرِ وَالصَّلٰوةِ وإنَّهَا لَكَبِيرَةٌ إلاَّ عَلَى الْخَاشِعِينَ.

> Seek help in patience and prayer *(ṣalāt)*, and truly it is hard except for the humble. (2:45)

Prayer in the context of this blessed verse is used in its literal meaning and denotes focusing attention on the Supreme Creator. Thus, patience, forbearance, and tolerating hardships with remembrance of God can ease difficulties and afflictions and are—in effect—important factors for triumph and salvation. Accordingly, it has been observed that those people who in daily life may cry from a simple wound to their hand, in the battlefield of struggle and fight against enemies of religion, are never afraid to loose an arm or a leg and never feel any fear or weakness in their heart. It is with this consideration in mind that the Immaculate Imāms, may God's peace and blessing be upon them all, have made frequent recommendations and astonishing exhortations concerning expedient dissimulation to the extent that they have considered its abandonment under certain circumstances as one of the capital sins.

One day Abū Baṣīr asked Ḥaḍrat-i Ṣādiq, "Can one see God on the day of Resurrection?" (That is because the Ashʿarites believe that in the Hereafter on the day of Resurrection all people will see God physically [by way of imagination and visualization, of course]). Exalted is God's Glory regardless of what the wrongdoers say! The Imām answered: "One can see Him in this world too, in the same way that you yourself saw God in this gathering." Abū Baṣīr said: "O son of the Messenger of Allāh do you allow me to narrate this for other people?" Ḥaḍrat Ṣādiq said: "Do not narrate this saying because the [common] people cannot understand its meaning and therefore will be misled."

Spiritual Master and Teacher (The Shaykh)

There are two categories of spiritual teacher and master. One is the teacher in its ordinary and universal term *(ustād-i ʿāmm);* the other is the particular teacher *(ustād-i khāṣṣ).* In the first context, a teacher is someone who is not especially chosen or appointed to guide others [in spiritual matters]. Seeking the advice of such a teacher falls in the broader context of Qur'ānic injunction to consult *those who are people of knowledge,* as is understood in accordance with the general meaning of the following verse:

فَاسْئَلُوا أَهْلَ الذِّكْرِ إِنْ كُنْتُمْ لاَ تَعْلَمُونَ.

Ask the people of the Remembrance if you do not know. (16:43)

The need to refer to an *ordinary* teacher is only at the initial stages of spiritual journey. However, when the traveler is honored by authentic visions and the theophany of Divine Attributes and Essence *(mushāhadāt wa tajallīyāt-i ṣifātīyah wa dhātīyah),* association with such a teacher is no longer necessary. As to the *particular* spiritual teacher and master, he is the one who is specifically designated to guide people in spiritual matters. They are the Prophet of Allāh [Muhammad], and his true and legitimate successors [i.e., the Shīʿite Imāms] and vicegerents. The wayfarer cannot dispense with the companionship of and attachment to the *particular* teacher under any circumstances even if he reaches his desired spiritual destination. Obviously, what is meant by attachment and companionship *(murāfaqat)*[14] is inward attachment and companionship of the Imām with the traveler, and not necessarily outward and physical association. Because the reality of the Imām is none other than the station of his luminosity that dominates over the world and its inhabitants. As to the Imām's corporeal being, even though it has its own nobility and grace in relation to other human beings, nonetheless, it is not the source of any consequence or particular efficacy or dispensation in the affairs of the universe.

To further clarify this point, it is important to mention that the source of all that which finds concrete existence and manifestation in the world of creation is the Divine Names and Attributes, and the reality of the Imām is the same as the Names and Attributes of God. Therefore, it is on the basis of this fact that the Imāms have said: "The wheel of the world of being, the heavens, and the entire universe turns by our hands and everything takes place with our sanction and permission":

بِنَا عُرِفَ اللَّهُ، بِنَا عُبِدَ اللَّهُ

> It is through us that God is known and it is through us that God is worshiped.

Accordingly, in the process of wayfaring, the traveler traverses within the planes of the Imām's luminosity. Any spiritual station he may ascend or status he may attain, the Imām already possesses and accompanies the wayfarer in that plane and station.

By the same token, the Imām's companionship and friendship is necessary even after the attainment of the desired spiritual goal of union *(wuṣūl)* with the Beloved, for it is he who must teach the traveler the rules and manners of the abode of Divine Names *(lāhūt)*. Therefore, companionship of the Imām in every situation is an important, and perhaps *the most important* condition and requirement of spiritual journey. There are profound mysteries to this fact that cannot be confined in words and description, but the traveler must discover them through discernment and intellectual intuition.

One day, Muḥyī al-Dīn [ibn al-]ʿArabī went to a spiritual master and complained about the spread of injustice and sin [on earth]. The teacher advised him to "Pay attention to your God." After some time, he went to another master and again complained about the increasing spread of sins and injustice. This time the teacher instructed him to "Pay attention to your own soul." Thereupon Ibn al-ʿArabī began to weep and asked the master the reasons for different replies he had received to the same question. The teacher answered: "O the apple of my eye! Both answers are the same. He invited you to the Friend *(rafīq)*, and I am inviting you to the Way *(ṭarīq)*."

We relate this story to demonstrate that wayfaring in the path of God and toward God is not in contradiction with wayfaring in the Divine Names and Attributes, which are essentially the same as the station of the Imām. They are very close to one another and are indeed identical. In that realm, there is no duality to be found; rather, whatever exists there is a single light, which is the Divine Light. Ultimately, that light is described in different terms at different times; sometimes as Divine Names and Attributes, and at other times as the reality or luminosity of the Imām.

عِبَارَاتُنَا شَتَّى وَحُسْنُكَ وَاحِدٌ   وَكُلٌّ إِلَى ذَاكَ الْجَمَالِ يُشِيرُ

Our descriptions are various,
but Thy Beauty is one,
it is to Thy Beauty
that all of them allude.

It is not possible to know the *ordinary* teacher and recognize his qualities except through one's association and companionship with him in public and private until his truthfulness and total certainty *(yaqīn)* are unequivocally proven to the traveler. One cannot find out whether a teacher has reached the station of union *(wuṣūl)* with the Beloved on the basis of such abilities as performing extraordinary and miraculous acts, possessing the knowledge of the hidden mysteries, mind reading, walking on fire and water, miraculous journeying over land and in the air *(ṭayy al-arḍ wa al-hawā')*, knowledge of the future and the past, and similar wondrous and eccentric acts, because all these faculties are acquired at the stage of unveiling of the spirit *(mukāshafa-yi rūhīyah)*. But there is a very long distance between this point and the stations of union and perfection *(kamāl).* Such a teacher cannot become a spiritual master so long as the theophanies of Lordly Essence *(tajallīyāt-i dhātīyah-i rabbānīyah)* are not manifested in him. One cannot rely merely on the theophanies of Divine Names and Attributes *(tajallīyyat-i ṣifātīyah wa asmā'īyah)* in a teacher and regard them as indications of his perfection and union [with the Beloved].

The meaning of the theophany of Divine Attributes *(tajallī-yi ṣifātī)* is that the traveler observes Divine Attributes in himself and regards his own knowledge, power, or life, as those of God. Thus, if he hears something he would perceive that it is God who hears it because *He is* the *All-Hearing (Samī');* when he sees something, he would understand that God sees it because *He is the All-Seeing (Baṣīr);* he would consider all knowledge of the world as God's, and would realize that the knowledge of all existence is derived from or is the same as God's knowledge.

The theophany of Divine Names *(tajallī-yi asmā'ī)* means that the wayfarer would observe in himself those Attributes of God that are supported by His Divine Essence, such as the Standing *(Qā'im),* the All-Knowing *('Alīm),* the All-Hearing *(Samī'),* the All-Seeing *(Baṣīr),* the Omnipotent *(Qādir),* and the like. For instance, he would come to realize that there is only One Knower in the world and that is God, Exalted is He; and that he would no longer consider himself as a knower before Him; rather, he would realize that his knowledge is in fact God's knowledge. Or he should understand that the Living One is one and that it is God, and that he himself is essentially not living, except in God. In the final analysis, the wayfarer should understand that There is no powerful, knower, and living being except God, Exalted and Holy is He.

لَيْسَ الْقَدِيرُ وَالْعَلِيمُ وَالْحَيُّ إلاَّ هُوَ تَعَالَى وَتَقَدَّسَ.

> The Almighty, the All-knowing and the Living One is none but He, Exalted, the Sacred.

Of course, it is possible that the theophany of Divine Names would be manifested in one's being in relation to certain Divine Names only. But manifestation of one Divine Name or two in a traveler does not necessarily mean that other Names would also be reflected in his being.

The theophany of Divine Essence *(tajallī-i dhātī)* is when God's Essence manifests Itself in the wayfarer's being; and that is attained only when he transcends all names and identities. In other words, this is possible only when he loses his *selfhood* totally and entirely and finds no trace of his *self* in the world of being, forgets *self* and *selfhood (khud wa khudīyat)* once and for all; and finally, experiences that

There is none there other than Allāh.

وَلَيْسَ هُنَاكَ إِلاَّ اللّٰهُ

At this point deviation and aberration is no longer possible for such a traveler. So long as an iota of selfhood remains in the traveler's heart, Satan is not disappointed and still hopes to deceive him and lead him astray. But when, with the power of Divine Grace, Exalted and Blessed is He, the wayfarer obliterates his identity and wipes out his selfhood, he enters into the realm of Divine Names *(lāhūt)* and into God's sanctuary *(ḥaram),* wears the attire of intimacy, and is honored and blessed with the theophanies of Divine Essence, only then will Satan go away and leave him alone. An *ordinary* teacher must attain this station of perfection [to become qualified as a master and guide a wayfarer]; otherwise, a wayfarer cannot surrender himself to just anyone [who claims spiritual authority] and be obedient to him.

هزار دام به هر گام این بیابان است

که از هزار هزاران یکی از آن نجهند

A thousand traps lie concealed in every step in this wilderness,
Of thousands and thousands [of passers by],
hardly one will be saved from them and find deliverance.

Therefore, one must not surrender oneself to any person who displays his [spiritual] commodities and makes claims to disclosure and witnessing. Of course, in cases where it is impossible or difficult to investigate the qualifications of a teacher or a *shaykh;* one must trust in God, examine whatever the teacher prescribes or instructs in light of the Book of God and the tradition of the Messenger of Allāh and the practices of the Immaculate Imāms, may God's benedictions and peace be upon them; and if he finds them in agreement, put them into practice. Otherwise, he should disregard them. Obviously, since such a traveler takes every step with reliance on and trust in God, Satan will not be able to dominate over him.

إِنَّهُ لَيْسَ لَهُ سُلْطَانٌ عَلَى الَّذِينَ آمَنُوا وَعَلَى رَبِّهِمْ يَتَوَكَّلُونَ إِنَّمَا سُلْطَانُهُ
عَلَى الَّذِينَ يَتَوَلَّوْنَهُ وَالَّذِينَ هُمْ بِهِ مُشْرِكُونَ.

> Verily, he [Satan] has no power over those who believe and put their trust in their Lord; for his [Satan's] power is only over those who take him [Satan] for their friend and who ascribe partners unto Him [Allāh]. (16:99–100)

Litany (Wird)

Wird consists of verbal invocations *(adhkār)* and litanies *(awrād)* (sing. *dhikr* and *wird*) the type and frequency of which are determined by the spiritual guide. For prayers and litanies are like medicines that are beneficial to some patients and harmful to some others. Sometimes it happens that a traveler engages in two kinds of invocations, one of which directs his attention to multiplicity and the other toward Unity. When they are recited together, they usually neutralize one another's effect and produce no result. Of course, the spiritual master's special permission is required for recitation of those litanies that require special sanction. However, recitation of generally sanctioned litanies does not need special permission.

There are four categories of litanies. [They include] manifested recollection with tongue often concentrating on the invocation without attention to its meaning *(dhikr-i jalī* or *qālibī);* and, silent or hidden invocation where attention is focused on the meaning *(dhikr-i khafī* or *qalbī).* Each of these two categories is either specific in number *(ḥaṣrī)* or nondelimited *(iṭlāqī).* The outward invocation is not very important in the eye of the people of the wayfaring, for it consists of verbal chanting often without particular attention to meaning. It is indeed the movement of the tongue *(laqlaqah-yi lisān)*. Since the traveler's quest is for nothing other than the inner meaning *(ma'nā)*, invocation with the tongue will be of no special efficacy and benefit for him.

Control of Incoming Thoughts (Naf-yi khawāṭir), Meditation (Fikr), and Invocation (Dhikr)

These three elements constitute important phases in reaching one's ultimate spiritual goal. Most people who fail to reach their spiritual destination stop in one of these three stages where they quit wayfaring permanently or become prone to going astray. There are many dangers in these phases, such as [turning toward] idolatry; worshiping stars, fire, and at times to atheism, pharaohism, claims of incarnation *(ḥulūl)*, and unification *(ittiḥād)* [with God]; renouncing obligatory rites; arbitrarily deciding what is permissible and what is forbidden by the *Sharī'ah (ḥalāl wa ḥarām)*; and other similar practices. Of course, we shall discuss all these dangers in due course. For the time being, however, we will examine two of the most important of those dangers, namely, incarnation *(ḥulūl)* and unification *(ittiḥād)*; dangers that the traveler will face as a result of purifying his mind through control and rejection of other incoming thoughts *(nafy-i khawāṭir)*.

Since the traveler has not yet transcended the realm of *selfhood* and personal identity when Divine Names and Attributes manifest themselves in him, he may fall into the trap of illusions and imagine that God has reached unity with him and his *self*—may God be our refuge. This meaning of incarnation and unification is indeed identical with heresey *(kufr)* and polytheism *(shirk)*; whereas the meaning of the concept of Unity of Being *(waḥdat al-wujūd)* essentially and totally negates multiplicity, otherness and distinctiveness, and regards all conceivable existents before God as passing shadows and illusions. When the traveler realizes the station of Unity of Being, he loses all his being, is denuded of his *selfhood* and is totally annihilated in God. As a result, he cannot intuitively sense any other existent in the world of existence except His Sacred Essence:

وَلَيْسَ فِي الدَّارِ غَيْرُهُ دَيَّارٌ.

There is no one in the house save Him [who is] the Landlord.

The difference and distance between this state and incarnation and union is from the earth to heaven.

The concept of control of the mind and rejecting incoming thoughts *(nafy-i khawāṭir)* denotes conquering the heart and governing over it so that it may not say something or commit an act, or be preoccupied with thoughts and memories except by the permission and will of its master. Achieving this state is an extremely difficult task, as it is said that thought control is one of the greatest purifiers of the inmost consciousness *(a'āẓim-i muṭahharāt-i sirr).* When the traveler sets out to practice controlling his thought, he realizes that a shattering flood of memories, thoughts, fantasies, and dreams overwhelms him. Even memories that he never imagined would come to his mind, such as past events or unreal thoughts, and imaginations enter his mind and totally capture and preoccupy him. In a situation like this, the wayfarer must remain firm like a majestic mountain, and with the sword of invocation cut off every thought that comes to his mind and causes distraction. In situations like this, invocation consists of none other than Divine Names, upon one of which the wayfarer must turn and focus his attention whenever his mind is distracted by those memories. He must meditate upon a particular Divine Name ceaselessly and focus upon it outwardly and inwardly (with his heart and his eye) until those memories are forced out of the abode of his heart. This is a very sound method to keep out thoughts solely with the help of *dhikr,* which is none other than remembrance of one of the Divine Names. God, Exalted is He, has said:

إِنَّ الَّذِينَ اتَّقَوْا إِذَا مَسَّهُمْ طَائِفٌ مِنَ الشَّيْطَانِ تَذَكَّرُوا فَإِذَا هُمْ مُبْصِرُونَ.

> Verily, those who fear God, when a visitation from Satan troubles them, they do but remember Allāh and behold them seers. (7:201)

In a treatise attributed to the late [Āyatullāh Sayyid Mahdī ibn Ḥasan] Baḥr al-'Ulūm[15] this practice has not been permitted. In that book, he strongly insists that control and rejection of incoming thoughts must be exercised without resorting to invocation. According to him, only when control is achieved over mind and thought, may one then start invocation of the Divine Names; for control and rejection of thoughts with the sword of invocation is an extremely dangerous enterprise. We shall briefly present his argumentation in the coming pages and then provide our own explanation and reason for its refutation. According to Baḥr al-ʿUlūm:

> Many spiritual masters teach [their disciples] that the process of thought control should be carried out with the help of invocation *(dhikr)*. Obviously, what is meant by invocation is meditation and concentration on the heart, and not verbal invocation for which the term litany *(wird)* is used. This is very dangerous. For the reality of the invocation consists of attention to the Beloved and concentration on His Beauty from a distance. The vision of the Beloved is permissible only when the eye is completely blind to anything other than Him; for the Beloved is jealous *(ghayūr)* and His jealousy *(ghayrat, Arabic ghayrah)* implies that it is not proper for the eye that sees Him to see anything other than Him. He will inflict with blindness any eye that turns away from Him to view someone or something else. Beholding Him while viewing other than Him is in conflict with His *ghayrah*. If seeing other than Him is repeated, it will amount to His contempt. The Beloved will respond by delivering such a strong blow on one's neck that he would lose both his hat and head.

وَمَنْ يَعْشُ عَنْ ذِكْرِ الرَّحْمَانِ نُقَيِّضْ لَهُ شَيْطَاناً فَهُوَ لَهُ قَرِينٌ.

> And he who is blind to the remembrance of the Beneficent, We assign unto him a Satan for companionship. (43:36)

Baḥr al-ʿUlūm nevertheless states that:

> only one kind of invocation is permissible in the process of practicing thought control; and that is the type of invocation whose objective is not to see the Beloved's Beauty, but to drive away the Satan, like a person who wants to expel an intruder from the meeting place with his beloved. In this case,

the purpose is to alarm and frighten the *stranger*. In such a case, the method used is that if a thought distracts the mind from concentration in such a manner that it becomes difficult to dispel it by other means, only then may one invoke Divine Names in order to expel those thoughts. However, the method used by those who have actualized their potentials on the Way and those conscious wayfarers who have attained the ultimate union [with the Beloved] is that in the process of teaching and guiding the novice, the spiritual guide should first instruct him to exercise mind control and then proceed to invocation. To teach mind control, such masters instruct the traveler to concentrate on a tangible object such as a stone or a piece of wood with one's inward and outward faculties and refrain as much as possible from blinking the eye. It is better that one practice this method continuously for forty days after the obligatory morning and night prayers and recite the threefold litanies of asking God for refuge *(isti'ādhah),* asking God for forgiveness *(istighfār),* and the formula, O Active *(Yā Fa'āl)* during that period. After this, the novice must focus on his heart and continue this practice for some time, concentrating on it fully and not allowing any other thought into his mind. Should any thought still distract his mind during the course of this practice, he should take recourse in the Divine Name *(Allāh)* and the formula "There is no existence except God" *(lā mawjūda ill'allāh).* The traveler must be persistent in this exercise until there emerges in his mind a quality of selflessness *(bīkhudī).*

Baḥr al-'Ulūm further recommends that

the appropriate prayer during this process is continuous recitation of the *istighfār* and *yā Fa'āl* formulae and the Divine Name O Expander *(yā Basīṭ).* When the wayfarer reaches this stage, he is then permitted to complete the remaining phases of thought control by imaginative silent invocation upon his soul *(dhikr-i nafsī-yi khayālī)* until his mind is totally cleansed and purified. Baḥr al-'Ulūm concludes that, God willing, preoccupation with memories and thoughts will gradually disappear as one advances further in the process of contemplation and invocation.

It should be known that this method of mind control that Baḥr al-ʿUlūm has mentioned here is adopted from the practice in the Naqshbandī order. The Naqshbandīs are a group of Sufis who are scattered in Turkey and some other places. The founder and spiritual guide *(murshid)* of the order was Khawājah Muhammad Naqshband, hence the name of the order, the Naqshbandīyyah.[16]

The approach of the late Ākhūnd Mullā Ḥusayn-Qulī Hamadānī, may God be pleased with him, was different. He and his disciples did not prescribe mind control without the practice of invocation. Rather, their method was based on constant attention and seriousness and attentiveness in different phases of it. Earlier we referred to this practice briefly. Here we shall discuss it in more detail.

The primary requirement of *murāqabah* for the traveler is to abstain from that which is forbidden by the *Sharīʿah (muḥarramāt),* and observe all obligatory religious duties *(wājibāt),* and never procrastinate in these matters. The second step is the intensification of *murāqabah,* wherein the traveler makes every effort to assure that his acts are for God's pleasure only, and to refrain from matters that are considered vain and frivolous. When he completes this stage; it will become a possibility for him and whereafter he will not be captured by anxiety or panic, and self-control will become his second nature *(malakah).*

The third phase of *murāqabah* is that the wayfarer constantly sees God with himself and watchful over him, and gradually realizes that God, the Almighty, is present and watchful everywhere and concerned about all creatures. This aspect of *murāqabah* must be observed in all states and at all times.

The fourth and final stage is a higher and more exalted one than the third stage. In this stage the traveler sees God's presence and in an undifferentiated manner observes Divine Beauty. These two latter stages of *murāqabah* are referred to in the advice of the Noble Prophet, may God's greetings and peace be upon him, to Abū Dhar Ghaffārī, may God be pleased with him:

أُعْبُدِ اللّٰهَ كَأَنَّكَ تَرَاهُ، فَإِنْ لَمْ تَكُنْ تَرَاهُ فَإِنَّهُ يَرَاكَ.

> Worship God as though you see Him, and if you do not see Him, He, nonetheless, sees you.

Accordingly, the merit of worship where God sees the wayfarer is less exalted than when he sees God.

When the traveler reaches this stage, in order to be able to expel everything other than God from his mind, thought control must be practiced when he is performing one of the rites of worship. For it is not permissible in the sacred *Sharīʿah* to concentrate on a stone or a piece of wood. If death were to descend to one in those moments, what kind of explanation would one have before God? However, control of incoming thoughts in the course of *dhikr* and with the weapon of invocation is an act of worship and is commended by the *Sharīʿah.* The best method of thought control is to focus on the soul, which is the fastest way to reach the intended goal. Because concentration on the soul is praised and accepted by the luminous *Sharīʿah,* as the noble verse indicates:

يَا أَيُّهَا الَّذِينَ آمَنُوا عَلَيْكُمْ أَنفُسَكُمْ لاَ يَضُرُّكُم مَّن ضَلَّ إِذَا اهْتَدَيْتُمْ.

> O you who believe, you have charge of your own souls. He who erred cannot harm you if you are rightly guided. (5:105)

The method of concentration on the soul was utilized and recommended by the late Ākhūnd Mullā Ḥusayn-Qulī. All his disciples followed this approach to gain knowledge of their souls *(maʿrifat al-nafs),* which is a prerequisite to acquiring knowledge of the Lord.

The reality of *gnosis (ʿirfān)* originates from Amīr al-Muʾminīn ʿAlī ibn Abī Ṭālib, may God's greetings be upon him. The number of orders that have accepted and spread this reality [his *wilāyah*] generation after generation and from masters to disciples exceeds more than one hundred. But the principal branches of *taṣawwuf* do not exceed twenty-five. All of these orders trace their origin to Ḥaḍrat ʿAlī ibn Abī Ṭālib, may God's greetings be upon him. Among these twenty-five orders, two or three belong to the *khāṣṣah* (i.e., Shīʿites) and all the rest belong to *ʿĀmmah* (i.e., Sunnis). Some of these orders also trace their origin to Imām Riḍā, may God's greetings be upon him, through Maʿrūf al-Karkhī. However, our order, which is the same as that of the late Ākhūnd (Mullā Ḥusayn Qulī), does not originate from and is not related to any of these chains *(silsilahs).*

Let us now turn to a brief discussion of our order. Over a hundred years ago there was an eminent scholar in the city of Shūshtar [in southern

Iran] named Āqā Sayyid ʿAlī Shūshtarī who held the function of the judge and religious authority for the people of Shūshtar. Like other prominent religious scholars of the time, he performed ordinary functions like teaching, judging, and settling disputes between people, and acting as a source of emulation *(marjaʿīyat-i taqlīd)* in religious matters. It has been reported that one day someone knocked at his door. When asked who it was, the visitor told him to open the door as he had business to conduct with him. When the late Āqā Sayyid ʿAlī opened the door, he saw a man whose appearance revealed that he was a weaver. When asked what he wanted, the weaver told him: "Such and such judgment that you had issued in favor of a person concerning the ownership of such and such property on the basis of the testimony of witnesses was not correct; and that the said property—in fact—belonged to a minor, an orphan." He then added that the deed of that property was buried in such and such location.

The weaver also told Sayyid ʿAlī Āqā that: "The path that you have adopted is not the right one; this path is not for you." Āyatullāh Shūshtarī asked the man whether he had committed any wrongdoing or followed the wrong way. The weaver replied: "I have already given my answer." Having said this the weaver went away. The Āyatullāh was immersed in his thought and wondered who that man was and what he had meant. After some investigation, it turned out that documents pertaining to the said property and proving the orphan's ownership of that were indeed buried in the same place as the weaver had indicated; and that the witnesses who had testified in favor of the other party had lied under duress and out of fear.

Sayyid Āqā ʿAlī became dismayed and wondered whether many of the judgments he had issued had been of this sort. He was overwhelmed by fear and anguish. The following night the weaver again knocked at his door and told him: "The true path is not the one on which you are traveling." The third night the same episode was repeated in precisely the same manner. This time the weaver also told him to sell his house and all his belongings as soon as possible, and go to the city of Najaf in Iraq and carry on the tasks that he will assign to him. Then he added that, "After six months, wait for me in the Wādī al-Salām cemetery in Najaf Ashraf."

Reportedly, the late Shūshtarī immediately began to carry out the weaver's instructions. He sold his house and gathered his belongings and made arrangements to depart for Najaf Ashraf. As soon as he arrived in

Najaf, at sunrise he saw the weaver in *Wādī al-Salām* cemetery standing in front of him as though he had come out of the ground. The weaver gave him some more instructions and disappeared. The late Āyatullāh took residence in Najaf Ashraf and carried out the weaver's instructions until he reached a station that words cannot describe. May God be pleased with him and may His peace be upon him.

In Najaf Ashraf, out of reverence for Shaykh Murtaḍā Anṣārī,[17] Āyatullāh Shūshtarī attended the Shaykh's lectures on jurisprudence *(fiqh)* and Principles *(uṣūl).* In return, Shaykh Anṣārī also went to Shūshtarī's class on ethics. When Shaykh Anṣārī, may God have mercy on him, passed away, Shūshtarī, may God have mercy on him, took charge of the Shaykh's chair and continued the lectures where the Shaykh had left. However, he did not live for very long and after six months departed toward God's eternal mercy. Once during that period, the late Shūshtarī sent a message to one of the most outstanding pupils of Shaykh Anṣārī, named Ākhūnd Mullā Ḥusayn-Qulī Dargazīnī Hamadānī. Hamadānī knew Shūshtarī while Shaykh Anṣārī was still alive and had benefited from his courses in ethics and gnosis. He planned to continue teaching the same subjects that Shaykh Anṣārī had taught, and had compiled the Shaykh's lectures and discourses. In that message Āyatullāh Shūshtarī reminded Hamadānī that that position (teaching) was not a perfect one for him, and that he should aim at attaining higher stations. This message transformed Hamadānī and guided him to the abode of the truth.

At any rate, the late Ākhūnd Hamadānī, who had studied sacred sciences under the late Āqā Sayyid ʿAlī several years before the death of the late Shaykh Anṣārī became one of the wonders of his time and superior to his contemporaries in the fields of ethics, spiritual struggle, and sacred sciences. Moreover, he trained several outstanding disciples, each of whom was considered a citadel of gnosis and a manifestation of Divine Unity. Among his most eminent pupils one can mention the late Ḥājj Mīrzā Jawād Āqā Malikī Tabrīzī, the late Āqā Sayyid Aḥmad Karbalāʾī Tihrānī, the late Āqā Sayyid Muhammad Saʿīd Ḥubbūbī, and the late Ḥājj Shaykh Muhammad Bahārī.

Our revered teacher and master, the unrivaled gnostic, the late Ḥājj Mīrzā ʿAlī Āqā Qāḍī Tabrīzī, may God be pleased with him, belonged to the circle of pupils of the late Āqā Sayyid Aḥmad Karbalāʾī. This is the chain *(silsilah)* of our masters and teachers that goes back to the late Āqā

ʿAlī Shūshtarī and ultimately to that weaver. As to the identity of the weaver and his connections or the source of his knowledge and instructions, nothing is known.[18]

Like our grand master and teacher Ākhūnd Mullā Ḥusayn-Qulī, the approach of our master and teacher the late Āqā Qāḍī Tabrīzī, was based on awareness and knowledge of the self *(maʿrifat al-nafs)*. In the initial stages, he always prescribed concentration on one's soul in order to gain control over mind and thought. According to his instruction, every day a novice traveler must devote a certain amount of time, half an hour or more, just to concentrate on his soul and practice to control his mind and thought. As a result of this concentration, slowly he would gain [spiritual] strength and thoughts and other mental preoccupations will disappear. Gradually, he would attain knowledge of his soul, and God willing, would ultimately reach his desired spiritual destination.

Most aspirants who have succeeded in liberating their mind and cleaning and purifying it from memories and ordinary preoccupations to prepare it for the rise of the Kingdom of Gnosis *(sulṭān-i maʿrifat),* have done so in one of the two following states. The first is during recitation of the Glorious Qurʾān, contemplating and wondering who the actual reciter of the Qurʾān is, and ultimately feeling [being revealed to] that the reciter is none other than God Himself, Majestic is His Glory.

Second is by pleading to *(tawassul)* and seeking the intercession of Ḥaḍrat Abā ʿAbd Allāh al-Ḥusayn, may God's blessing and peace be upon him, because he is graciously instrumental in lifting the veil and removing the obstacles on the path of God for the wayfarer.

As was mentioned in our discussion in previous pages, two factors play important parts in the theophany of the Kingdom of Gnosis. The first is constant attention *(murāqabah)* in its various forms and degrees of intensity; and second is concentration on the soul. When the traveler makes every effort to focus his attention on these two principles, gradually he will realize that the multiplicities of this world originate from and are nurtured by one wellspring, and anything that finds existence in the world derives its existence from one source. Any degree of light, beauty, glory, and perfection that may be present in any existing thing is derived from that single source that gives it the light of life, beauty, and majesty in accordance with its inherent capability *(qābilīyat-i māhuwī)*. In other words, absolute and boundless grace emanates unconditionally from the Absolute

Source and every existent receives its share in accordance with its qualifications and quiddity *(māhīyat).*

In any case, as a result of constant attention and persistent effort, gradually four [spiritual] realms will be revealed to the traveler.

The first realm is the world of Unity in deeds *(tawḥīd-i af'āl).* That is, at first the traveler realizes that whatever his eyes see, his tongue says, his ears hear, his feet, hands, and other bodily organs perform are all supported by his own soul, and the soul does what it wills. Then he realizes that whatever actions that take place in the external world derive from and are supported by himself. In other words, his soul is the source of all his [external] acts. Soon, however, he realizes that his soul subsists in the Divine Being and is only a gate for emanation of Divine Mercy and Grace; and therefore, all acts in the external world are supported by His Sacred Being.

The second realm is the world of Unity of Attributes *(Tawḥīd-i Ṣifāt)* and is revealed after the first realm. In this realm when the traveler hears, he does not regard the reality of hearing to belong to himself, but to God. Similarly, whatever he sees with his eyes, he perceives the reality of his sight as belonging to God. In short, he realizes that every kind of knowledge, power, life, hearing, sight, and everything else that he notices in the existent things in the external world all emanate from and subsist in God, Exalted is He.

The third realm is the world of Unity of Names *(Tawḥīd-i Asmā')* and it emerges after the second world. In this realm, the traveler understands that [Divine] Attributes subsist in His Essence. For example, he realizes that only God, Exalted is He, is the [real] Knower *('Ālim),* the Powerful *(Qādir),* and the Living *(Ḥayy).* In other words, he realizes that his own knowledge is, in fact, God's knowledge; and believes that his power, hearing, and sight all belong to God and are in God. In general, he understands that in the entire universe there is only One who is Powerful, Knowing, Seeing, and Living and that is God, Glorious is He; and that every existent thing, in proportion to its own existential reality, alludes to and reflects a certain degree of the reality of the *All-Knowing,* the *All-Powerful,* the *All-Hearing,* the *All-Seeing,* and the *Living.*

The fourth realm is the world of Unity of Essence *(Tawḥīd dar Dhāt),* which is higher than the third realm and is revealed to the wayfarer through the theophany of the Divine Essence. That is to say, the traveler realizes that the Essence by which all acts, attributes, and names are supported is One

Essence and One Reality in which they all subsist. At this point, the wayfarer is no longer concerned about Attributes and Names but solely with the Essence. This is realized only when he bids farewell to and leaves behind his derivative existence *(wujūd-i ʿāriyah wa majāzī)* and loses his identity and *selfhood* once and for all and annihilates them in the Sacred Essence of God, Exalted is He. This is the point of the theophany of the Essence. Of course, to name this station as the station of the Essence *(maqām-i dhāt),* the reality of the Essence *(ḥaqīqat-i dhāt),* or Unicity *(aḥadīyat)* or any other name is a waste of time and a meaningless and futile effort. For whatever can be expressed by the tongue or written by the pen is not beyond definition. Whereas the Sacred Divine Essence is above all definitions. One cannot find a proper name or description for It, nor can It be conceived in terms of states and stations. In fact, it is even beyond the boundaries of inability, for while inability implies negation, it still sets a limit for Him, and God the Almighty is above all limitations. When the traveler enters this realm, he loses his own identity and *selfhood.* He will not know himself, nor will he recognize any other person. In short, he will not know anyone except God, because ultimately only God can know Himself.

In the process of his journey in each of the fourfold realms, the traveler loses a part of his identity and selfhood—ultimately losing his total being and existence. In the first abode where he reaches the station of annihilation in the Act, he realizes that it is not he, but God, who acts. He loses all signs of his effects pertaining to action. In the second realm, thanks to the theophany of Divine Attributes, the traveler understands that knowledge, power, and all other qualities are exclusive to the Divine Essence, Glorious and Exalted. At this point he loses his own attributes and no longer sees any trace of them in himself. In the third realm, as a result of the theophany of the Divine Names, the traveler understands that it is God, the Glorious, who is the Knower and the Powerful. Here he loses his names and no longer finds them in himself. Finally, in the fourth abode, which is the realm of the theophany of Essence, the wayfarer loses his own existence and dispossesses his essence. He no longer sees himself, for the only essence that he sees is the Sacred Essence of God.

This phase of witnessing, that is, the theophany of the Essence, is referred to by gnostics as the Griffin *(ʿAnqā)* or *(Sīmurgh),* a mythical bird that no hunter can trap. The *Sīmurgh* is that Pure Essence and Absolute Being, which is called variously the world of Non-Being *(ʿālam-i ʿamāʾ),* the Hidden Treasure *(kanz-i makhfī),* the Invisible of all invisibles *(ghayb al-ghuyūb),* and the Essence that has no name and no identity *(dhāt mā lā isma lahū wa lā rasma lahū).*

برواین دام برمرغ دگَرنه

که عنقا رابلند است آشیانه

For another bird, go and set this snare,
for the Griffin has a nest on inaccessible heights.

It is interesting to see how well Ḥāfiẓ, may God's mercy be upon him, described this profound [metaphysical] truth in his poetry and explained it in such a powerful metaphorical fashion in the following *mathnawī:*

الا آهوی وحشی کجایی

مرا با توست چندین آشنایی

دوتنها و دو سرگَردان، دوبی کس

دد و دامت کمین ازپیش و ازپس

بیا تا حال یکدیگَر بدانیم

مراد هم بجوییم ارتوانیم

چنینم هست یاد ازپیر دانا

فراموشم نشد هرگَز همانا

که روزی رهروی در سرزمینی

به لطفش گَفت رندی ره نشینی

که ای سالك چه در انبانه داری

بیا دامی بنه گَر دانه داری

جوابش داد کآری دام دارم
ولی سیمرغ می باید شکارم
بگفتا گرچه این امری محال است
ولیکن نا امیدی هم و بال است
نکرد آن همدم دیرین مدارا
مسلمانان مسلمانان خدا را
مگر خضر مبارك پی تواند
که این تنها بدان تنها رساند

Lo! Wild gazelle, tell me where you are?
I have had with you much intimacy.
Two lonely and friendless wanderers in wilderness
Wild beasts and snares lying in ambush up and down the way.
Come, let us learn each other's plight,
And if we can, fulfill each other's dreams and wishes
So do I remember the old sage's words,
Which I have never forgotten:
That once a traveler in a certain land,
Was told in a subtle way by a wandering begger,
'O traveler what is it that thou carriest in thy bag,
Come and set a snare if thou hast any grain.'
He replied, 'Yes I do have a net,
But I must the Griffin hunt.'
He said, 'How shall you find its trace,
For it is traceless and traceless is its nest.'
He said, 'Though it should be an impossible task,
But despair too is a calamity.'
That old companion did not tolerate,
For God's sake! O Muslims! O Muslims!
Perhaps the Khiḍr, the blessed one will help,
For he alone can guide this lonely one to the Lonely One.

Obviously, when the Griffin's nest is traceless one cannot hope to hunt the Griffin itself, unless when His Grace becomes the guide and leads the wanderers of the abode of love and the lovers of His eternal Beauty into the realm of Unity and annihilation *(wādī-yi tawḥīd wa fanā')*. For the sake of the precursors of the abode of love, the standard bearers on the path of praise and Divine Knowledge *(ḥamd wa ma'rifah)*, Muhammad al-Muṣṭafā and 'Alī al-Murtaḍā and his eleven glorious sons in the descent of the Pure, Fāṭimah al-Zahrā'—may the peace of Allāh, the Exalted Sovereign, be upon them—O God, grant success to all your lovers and to us, to attain everything which pleases You and to join us with the Righteous Ones *(ṣāliḥīn)*.

Praise be to God for his generosity, this noble treatise, which has been named Kernel of the Kernel Concerning the Wayfaring and Spiritual Journey of the People of Intellects *(Risāla-yi lubb al-lubāb dar sayr wa sulūk-i ulu'l-albāb)* and which was completed by the pen of this nondescript and poor being on the eighth night of the month of fasting in the year 1369 of Hijrah (June 24, 1950).

وَلَهُ الْحَمْدُ فِي الأُولَى وَالآخِرَةِ، وَآخِرُ دَعْوَانَا أَنِ الْحَمْدُ لِلَّهِ رَبِّ الْعَالَمِينَ.

And to Him belongs all Praise, in the World and the Hereafter. May our last call be *alhamduli'llah rabb al-'ālamīn* (All Praise belongs to God, the Lord of this world and the next).

This nondescript and poor being is Sayyid Muhammad Ḥusayn Ḥusaynī Tihrānī, at the holy city of Qum.

Notes

1. This narration is reported in Kulaynī, *Uṣūl al-Kāfī*, 2: 45.
2. This is perhaps an allusion to the story about the Prophet's mosque where he used to lean on a column and deliver the sermons before daily prayers. It is narrated that when a pulpit was built for the Prophet (peace be upon him) and he began to use that for delivering

his sermons, he heard someone crying and mourning in the background in utmost sadness. When he looked around, he noticed that it was that column which was mourning and crying because of separation from him. In his *Mathnawī,* Jalāl al-Dīn Rūmī narrates this story in the following poem:

استن حنانه از هجر رسول   ناله میزد همچو ارباب عقول
در میان مجلس وعظ آنچنان   کز وی آکَه کَشت هم پیرو جوان
دِر تحیر مانده اصحاب رسول   کِز چه مینالد ستون با عرض وطول
کَفت پیفمبر چه خواهي ای ستون   کَفت جانم از فراغت کشت خون
از فراق تو مرا چون سوخت جان   چون ننالم بی تو ای جان جهان
مسندت من دودوم از من تاختی   بر سر منبر تو مسند ساختی

The column crying from the pain of separation
from the Messenger,
cried like people of intellect,
In the middle of the Prophet's Sermon,
so bitterly that the young and the old noticed.
Puzzled were the Messenger's companions wondering why,
was the column crying with all its being?
O column, "What do you want?" said the Prophet,

"My soul is drowned in the blood of sadness
because of separation from you,"
answered the column.
"Being separated and far away from you
How can I not cry, O! soul of the universe,
When my soul is burning from the pain of your separation,"
"I was your seat, you went away from me,
and made your sitting place on the pulpit. . . ."

See Jalāl al-Dīn Rūmī, *Mathnawī-yi ma'nawī,* edited with an introduction and commentary by Ḥājj Muhammad Ramaḍānī, 6th ed., Tehran, 1366/1997, Book I, pp. 43–44.

3. Kulaynī, *Uṣūl al-Kāfī,* 2:453

4. This poem is attributed to majnūn al-ʿĀmirī and is available in, *Jāmīʿ al-shawāhid* (Tehran, 1270h/1850, lithograph ed.)
5. Ḥājj Mīrzā Jawād Āqā Malikī Tabrīzī, *Risāla-yi laqāʾ Allāh* (n.d.)
6. Some consider these the fourfold veils that seprate the wayfarer from the Beloved, hence the fourfold stations. Renouncing the world, the hereafter, anything other than God, and renouncing renunciation *(tark-i dunyā, tark-i ʿuqbāʾ, tark-i mawlāʾ, tark-i tark.)*
7. Kulaynī, *Uṣūl al-Kāfī,* 2:113. See also Muhammad Bāqir Majlisī, *Biḥār al-Anwār,* 15:186.
8. *Biḥār al-Anwār,* 15:186.
9. Ibid., 15:184.
10. Narrated in Shaykh Jaʿafar Kashfī, *Tuḥfat al-mulūk.*
11. God, exalted is He, addressed the Prophet, peace be upon him, in the following terms: "O Aḥmad, have only one concern, a single [invoking] tongue, keep your being conscious, and do not be negligent of me." See Majlisī, *Biḥār al-Anwār,* 17:8–9.
12. Salmān Fārsī was the first Persian to accept Islām and one of the closest companions of the Prophet.
13. *Taqīyah* means expedient dissimulation. It literally means one protecting oneself in face of danger. Some scholars translated it as *"counsel of caution"* on the part of a persecuted minority. See Ḥamīd ʿEnāyat, *Modern Islamic Political Thought* (Austin: University of Texas Press), 1982, p. 175.
14. At every age, there may exist numerous Friends of God *(Awliyāʾ Allāh)* who have attained perfection and are qualified to provide spiritual guidance to aspiring wayfarers. However, at any given age, there is only one Pole/Imām under whose spiritual authority *(wilāyah)* are all friends of God and in whose name they provide guidance. It is necessary for the wayfarer to focus on him and feel his presence. This is what is meant by companionship *(murāfaqat).* The term "Particular Teacher" *(ustād-i khāṣṣ)* refers to this authority. In Shīʿism, during the period of Greater Occultation this authority belongs exclusively to the twelfth Imām (May God's greetings be upon him). See ʿAllāmah Tihrānī's comments on Baḥr al-ʿUlūm's *Ṛisāla-yi Sayr wa Sulūk,* pp. 166–167, n. 137.
15. Sayyid Mahdī ibn Sayyid Murtaḍā al-Ṭabāṭabāʾī al-Najafī known as Baḥr al-ʿUlūm, *Risāla-yi Sayr wa Sulūk* (Treatise on Wayfaring and Spiritual Journey), edited with an introduction and commentary by

Āyatullāh Sayyid Muhammad Ḥusayn Ḥusaynī Tihrānī, 3d. ed. (Mashhad: 1417/1995).

16. On Naqshbandī order see K. A. Niẓāmī, "The Nashbandīyah Order" in Seyyed Hossein Nasr (ed.) (*Islamic Spirituality: Manifestation*, New York, 1991), pp. 162–193.
17. Shaykh Murtaḍā Anṣārī (d. 1281/1864) was the most prominent Shīʿite scholar and the *marjaʿi taqlīd* (Supreme Source of Emulation) in the nineteenth century (d. 1281 A.H./1864). Among his many works one can cite *Farāʾiḍ al-uṣūl* (Qum,1987), *al-Makāsib* (Tabriz: 1955), and *Ṣirāṭ al-najāt* (Tehran: lithograph edition, 1290/1873).
18. This is an allusion to the initiatic authority of the Hidden (twelfth) Imām, *Ḥaḍrat Ḥujjat ibn Ḥasan al-ʿAsgarī* (May God's greetings be upon him). It is believed that He appears from time to time to initiate certain individuals of exceptional spiritual realization, without revealing his true identity.

INDEX OF QUR'ĀNIC VERSES

INDEX OF AḤĀDĪTH

جَذْبَةٌ مِنْ جَذَبَاتِ الرَّحْمَنِ تُوَازِي عِبَادَةَ الثَّقَلَيْنِ

1. A single attraction from God, the Most Compassionate, outbalances the worship of all men and *jinn.*

مَنْ أَخْلَصَ لِلَّه أَرْبَعِينَ صَبَاحاً ظَهَرَتْ يَنَابِيعُ الْحِكْمَةِ مِنْ قَلْبِهِ إِلَى لِسَانِهِ.

2. Whoever sincerely purifies his heart for God for forty days will find springs of wisdom gush forth from his heart and flow toward his tongue.

كَانَ اللَّهُ وَلَمْ يَكُنْ مَعَهُ شَيءٌ

3. God was, and there was nothing else besides Him.

لِي مَعَ اللَّهِ حَالاَتٌ لاَ يَسَعُهَا مَلَكٌ مُقَرَّبٌ

4. Inwardly I have such exalted states with God which no angel brought nigh encompasses.

أَنَا بَشَرٌ مِثْلُكُمْ

5. I am only a mortal human being like you.

لَوْلاَ تَكْثِيرٌ فِي كَلاَمِكُمْ، وَتَمْرِيجٌ فِي قُلُوبِكُمْ لَرَأَيْتُمْ مَا أَرَى، وَلَسَمِعْتُمْ مَا أَسْمَعُ.

6. Were it not for loquacity of your sayings and temptations and anxiety in your hearts, you would indeed see what I see and hear what I hear.

لَوْلاَ أنَّ الشَّيَاطِينَ يَحُومُونَ حَوْلَ قُلُوبِ بَنِي آدَمَ لَرَأوْا مَلَكُوتَ السَّمَاوَاتِ وَالأرْضِ.

7. Were it not for the devils surrounding the hearts of the children of Adam, they would witness the Kingdom *(malakūt)* of the Heavens and the Earth.

أنْتَ فِي أظْلَمِ العَوَالِمِ

8. You are in the darkest of the [Divine] realms.

نَحْنُ مَعَاشِرَ الأنْبِيَاءِ اُمِرْنَا أنْ نُكَلِّمَ النَّاسَ عَلَى قَدْرِ عُقُولِهِمْ.

9. We [the prophets] have been commanded to speak to the people in accordance with the level of their intellects.

الإحسَانُ أنْ تَعْبُدَ اللّهَ كَأنَّكَ تَرَاهُ، وَإنْ لَمْ تَكُنْ تَرَاهُ فَانَّهُ يَرَاكَ

10. Iḥsān is to adore Allāh as though thou didst see Him, and if thou dost not see Him, He nonetheless seeth you.

أعْدَى عَدُوِّكَ نَفْسُكَ الَّتِي بَيْنَ جَنْبَيْكَ.

11. Your most ardent enemy is your carnal soul, which dwells between your two sides.

اَللَّهُمَّ إنِّي أعُوذُ بِكَ مِنَ الشِّرْكِ الْخَفِيِّ.

12. O God, I seek Thy refuge from hidden polytheism *(shirk al-khafy).*

مَنْ أرَادَ أنْ يَنْظُرَ إلَى مَيِّتٍ يَمْشِي فَلْيَنْظُرْ إلَى عَلِيِّ بْنِ أبِي طَالِبٍ.

13. Whoever wishes to see a walking dead man, he should look at ʿAlī ibn Abī Ṭālib.

الايمَانُ لاَ يَكُونَ إلاَّ بِالْعَمَلِ، وَالْعَمَلُ مِنْهُ، وَلاَ يَثْبُتُ الايمَانُ إلاَّ بِالْعَمَلِ.

14. Faith cannot be [actualized] without action, and action is a part of faith. Faith will not be established except with action.

إِلَهِي أَسْأَلُكَ حُبَّكَ وَحُبَّ مَنْ يُحِبُّكَ

15. O my God, I beseech you to grant me Your love and the love of those who love you.

INDEX OF QUOTATIONS OF THE SAYINGS OF THE SHĪʿITE IMĀMS

اَللّٰهُمَّ نَوِّرْ ظَاهِرِي بِطَاعَتِكَ، وَبَاطِنِي بِمَحَبَّتِكَ، وَقَلْبِي بِمَعْرِفَتِكَ،
وَرُوحِي بِمُشَاهَدَتِكَ، وَسِرِّي بِاسْتِقْلَالِ اتِّصَالِ حَضْرَتِكَ، يَا ذَا الْجَلَالِ
وَالإِكْرَامِ.

O God, illuminate my outward with [the light] of obedience to Thee and my inner being with Thy love, my heart with the knowledge of Thee, my spirit with thy vision, and my inmost consciousness *(sirr)* with the independence of attachment to Thy Threshold, O Lord of Majesty and Munificence. (Imām ʿAlī, Nahj al Balāghah)

نَحنُ أَسْمَاءُ اللّٰه.

We are the Names of God.

إِنَّ الإِسْلَامَ هُوَ التَّسْلِيمُ، وَالتَّسْلِيمُ هُوَ الْيَقِينُ.

Verily Islām means submission, and submission means certainty. (Imām ʿAlī)

أَرْكَانُ الْكُفْرِ أَرْبَعَةٌ: الرَّغْبَةُ وَالرَّهْبَةُ وَالسُّخْطُ وَالْغَضَبُ.

The pillars of heresy are four: desire, fear, anger, and rage. (Imām Ṣādiq)

أَبْصَرَ طَرِيقَهُ، وَسَلَكَ سَبِيلَهُ، وَعَرَفَ مَنَارَهُ، وَقَطَعَ غِمَارَهُ، فَهُوَ مِنَ
الْيَقِينِ عَلَى مِثْلِ ضَوْءِ الشَّمْسِ.

. . . who has seen his way, has traversed his path, has recognized its minaret, has removed its veils. He has attained a degree of certainty which is like the certainty of the rays of the sun. (Nahj al-Balāghah)

هَجَمَ بِهِمِ الْعِلْمُ عَلَى حَقِيقَةِ الْبَصِيرَةِ، وَبَاشَرُوا رُوحَ الْيَقِينِ، وَاسْتَلاَنُوا مَا اسْتَوْعَرَهُ الْمُتْرَفُونَ، وَأَنِسُوا بِمَا اسْتَوْحَشَ مِنْهُ الْجَاهِلُونَ، وَصَحِبُوا الدُّنْيَا بِأَبْدَانٍ أَرْوَاحُهَا مُعَلَّقَةٌ بِالْمَحَلِّ الأَعْلَى.

. . . Knowledge of the truth of discernment descends upon them from all directions, and the spirit of certainty becomes their companion. That which seems harsh and difficult to the spoiled souls, becomes smooth and easy to them. They become intimate with what the ignorant is afraid of. They are confined in bodies in this world while their spirits dwell on highest realms of the Kingdom [of God]. (Nahj al-Balāghah)

يَا عَبْدَ الْعَزِيزِ إِنَّ لِلإِيمَانِ عَشْرَ دَرَجَاتٍ بِمَنْزِلَةِ السُّلَّمِ يُصْعَدُ مِنْهُ مِرْقَاةً بَعْدَ مِرْقَاتٍ إِلَى أَنْ قَالَ عليه السلام وَإِذَا رَأَيْتَ مَنْ هُوَ أَسْفَلُ مِنْكَ بِدَرَجَةٍ فَارْفَعْهُ إِلَيْكَ بِرِفْقٍ، وَلاَ تَحْمِلَنَّ عَلَيْهِ مَا لاَ يُطِيقُ فَتَكْسِرَهُ.

Verily there are ten levels for faith and it is like a ladder which must be climbed one step at a time. When you see someone who is a step lower than you are, lift him up gently to yourself, and do not impose a burden upon him which he cannot stand and that will break him. (Imām Ṣādiq)

وَلاَ تُكْرِهُوا عَلَى أَنْفُسِكُمُ الْعِبَادَةَ.

Do not impose worship upon your soul with reluctance. (Imām Ṣādiq)

لَيْسَ مِنَّا مَنْ لَمْ يُحَاسِبْ نَفْسَهُ كُلَّ يَوْمٍ مَرَّةً.

He who does not scrutinize the account of his own soul once every day is not one of us. (Imām Mūsā Kāẓim)

الْعُبَّادُ ثَلاَثَةٌ: قَوْمٌ عَبَدُوا اللَّهَ خَوْفاً فَتِلْكَ عِبَادَةُ الْعَبِيدِ، وَقَوْمٌ عَبَدُوا اللَّهَ
طَمْعاً فَتِلْكَ عِبَادَةُ الأُجَرَاءِ، وَقَوْمٌ عَبَدُوا اللَّهَ حُبّاً فَتِلْكَ عِبَادَةُ الأَحْرَارِ.

Worshipers are of three categories: Those who worship God out of Fear (that is the worship of slaves and bondsmen); those who worship Him out of greed (that is the worship of merchants); and finally, those who worship Him out of love, and this is the worship of free-spirited men [i.e., gnostics *('urafā')*]. (Imām Ṣādiq)

إِنَّ شِيعَتَنَا الْخُرْسُ.

Surely, our followers are the mute ones. (Imām Ṣādiq)

الصَّمْتُ شِعَارُ الْمُحِبِّينَ، وَفِيهِ رِضَا الرَّبِّ، وَهُوَ مِنْ أَخْلاَقِ الأَنْبِيَاءِ
وَشِعَارِ الأَصْفِيَاءِ.

Silence is the motto of lovers [of God], and in it lies the Lord's pleasure. It is the virtue of the prophets and the motto of the pure ones. (Imām Ṣādiq)

الصَّمْتُ شِعَارُ الْمُحِبِّينَ، وَفِيهِ رِضَا الرَّبِّ، وَهُوَ مِنْ أَخْلاَقِ الأَنْبِيَاءِ
وَشِعَارِ الأَصْفِيَاءِ.

Silence is a gate from among the gates of wisdom, and it is indeed the guide to every good. (Imām Riḍā)

الْجُوعُ إِدَامُ الْمُؤْمِنِ، وَغِذَاءُ الرُّوحِ، وَطَعَامُ الْقَلْبِ.

Hunger is the believer's condiment, the spirit's nourishment, and the heart's food. (Imām Ṣādiq)

وَاسْتَعِينُوا بِالصَّبْرِ وَالصَّلَوةِ وإِنَّهَا لَكَبِيرَةٌ إِلاَّ عَلَى الْخَاشِعِينَ.

> Seek help in patience and prayer *(ṣalāt),* and truly it is hard except for the humble. (2:45)

One day I (Abū Baṣīr) asked Ḥaḍrat Ṣādiq, may peace be upon him, "Can one see God on the day of Resurrection?" (That is because the Ash'arites believe that in the Hereafter on the Day of Resurrection all people will see God physically [metaphorically of course]. Exalted is God's Glory despite what the wrongdoers say). The Imām answered, "Yes. One can see Him even before the Day of Judgment in this world too." I said how? He said "When God told them 'Am I not your Lord' and they said yes." The Imām was silent for a moment and then said: "Verily the faithful believers will see Him in this world before the Day of Judgment in the same way that you yourself are seeing God in this gathering." Abū Baṣīr said I said to him O son of the Messenger of Allāh, do you permit me to narrate this for other people? Ḥaḍrat Ṣādiq said, "Do not narrate this saying because the [ordinary] people cannot understand the meaning of what is said and therefore they will be misled and then will think that this statement is heretical. Of course seeing by heart is not like seeing by eye. Exalted is God from whatever He is compared to by unbelievers."

The above narration is mentioned by [Abū Ja'far Muhammad ibn Bābūyah, known as] al-Shaykh Ṣadūq in the *Book of Unity (Kitāh al-Tawḥīd)* on the question of one's ability to see God *(raw'yat).* The chain of transmission goes back to Abū Baṣīr himself who had taken this question to Imām Ṣādiq, may God's greetings be upon him.

بِنَا عُرِفَ اللّٰهُ، بِنَا عُبِدَ اللّٰهُ

It is through us that God is known and it is through us that God is worshiped. (Imām Ṣādiq)

NOTES ON SAINTS, SCHOLARS, AND AUTHORS CITED IN THE TEXT

1. 'Alī ibn Abī Ṭālib (578 B.H.–40 A.H. /598–661): The cousin and son-in-law of the Prophet, the first Imām of the Shī'ites, and the fourth Caliph.
2. 'Alī ibn Mūsā al-Riḍā: The eighth Imām of the Shī'ites who was chosen by al-Ma'mūn as his heir-apparent and is considered as the Imām of Initiation.
3. Anṣārī, Muhammad Jawād (d. 1379 A.H. /1961): One of the most outstanding Shī'ī religious scholars who studied and taught in Najaf. Later in life, he settled in Hamadān at the age of fifty-nine. He taught 'Allāmah Tihrānī the doctrinal foundations of gnosis and had an important role in his spiritual life.
4. Bābā Farajūllāh Majdhūb: A prominent Sufi master from Adharbaijān who lived in the early part of the twentieth century.
5. Baḥr al-'Ulūm, Sayyid Mahdī: (1155–1212 A.H./1742–1797): Born in Karbalā', he was one of the most important Shī'ī 'ulamā of Iraq and was widely recognized as the most knowledgeable scholar of his time, hence the title *Baḥr al-'Ulūm* (Ocean of knowledge).
6. al-Ghazzālī, Muhammad (d. 505 A.H./1111): Muslim theologian, philosopher, and thinker who is particularly famous for writing such monumental works as *Iḥyā' 'Ulūm al-Dīn, Tuhāfat al-falāsafah,* and, *Kimiyā-yi Sa'ādat* (in Persian).
7. Ḥaddād, Ḥājj Sayyid Hāshim (d. 1404 A.H./1983): The most distinguished gnostic in Najaf and the spiritual master and guide of 'Allāmah Tihrānī. He passed away in Mashhad in 1983.
8. Ḥāfiẓ, Shams al-Dīn Muhammad (726–792/1317–1392): also called *lisān al-ghayb*. Persian scholar, thinker, and the greatest Persian Sufi poet who has reflected the most profound Divine mysteries in his poetry.
9. Hamadānī, Ākhūnd Mullā Ḥusaynqulī: Islamic scholar and Sufi master who taught in Najaf and trained more than 300 students including

such outstanding scholars and mystics as Sayyid Aḥmad Karbalā'ī, Ḥājj Mīrzā Javād Āqā Malikī Tabrīzī, Shaykh Muhammad Bahārī, and Sayyid Muhammad Ḥubbūbī.

10. Ḥusayn ibn ʿAlī: The third Shīʿī Imām who was martyred in Karbalā' in 61 A.H./680 in a battle against the Umayyid Caliph Yazīd ibn Muʿāwiyah.
11. Ḥusaynī Tihrānī, Ḥājj Sayyid Ibrāhim: Grandfather of ʿAllāmah Tihrānī.
12. Ibn Fāriḍ, ʿUmar: (d. 632 A.H./1235). One of the most eminent Arab Sufi-poets whose *Poems of the Path (naẓm al-sulūk)* is widely read and taught in religious schools in Qum and Mashhad.
13. Ibn Sīnā (Avicenna 428–79/980–1037): One of the most prominent Muslim philosophers who was also a well-known physician. Among his many works are *Shifā'*, *Qānūn*, and *Risālah fi mabda' wa al-maʿād.*
14. Jaʿ afar ibn Ṣādiq: (d. 148 A.H./765) The sixth Shīʿī Imām and the founder of the Jaʿafarī school of law who is widely recognized as an authority on Islamic law and sciences by Sunnis and Shīʿīs alike.
15. Jīlī, Shaykh ʿAbd al-Karīm: the eminent Sufi master, student of the school of ibn al-ʿArabī, and the author of *al-Insān al-kāmil.* Translated by Titus Burckhardt as *De l' homme universal,* Lyons, 1953.
16. Karbalā'ī, Sayyid Aḥmad: A student of Mullā Ḥusaynqulī Hamadānī and the spiritual guide and master of Ḥājj Sayyid ʿAlī Qāḍī
17. Khātūn Ābādī, Sayyid Muhammad Ṣāliḥ: The author of *waqāi'yʿ al-sanīn wa al-ayyām.*
18. Khiḍr: The prophet who is believed to be immortal and can initiate sincere aspirants into the Divine mysteries. In the context of Shīʿism, he is believed to correspond to the Hidden Imām who is the Quṭb (Pole) of the Universe.
19. Khu'ī, Ḥājj Abu'l-Qāsim: One of the most outstanding Shīʿī -Iranian scholars and religious leaders of the twentieth century who was a Supreme Source of Emulation *(marjaʿ-i taqlīd).* He spent most of his life in the shrine cities of Iraq where he taught and guided people until his death in 1995. He was particularly known for establishing and overseeing an extensive network of charity organization with branches in the Muslim world and Europe.
20. Mīr Dāmād, Sayyid Muhammad: (d. 1040/1630) Prominent theosopher, religious scholar, logician, and mystic of the Safavid period who founded the School of Isfahan. He created a harmony between the

cosmology of Avicenna and Shīʿite imamology, and trained many outstanding students including Ṣadr al-Dīn Shīrāzī, known as Mullā Ṣadrā.

21. Mūsā al-Kāẓim (d. 179 A.H./795): The seventh Shīʿī Imām who was imprisoned by the ʿAbbāsid Caliph Hārūn al-Rashīd for about thirteen years.
22. Muṭahharī, Āyatullāh Murtaḍā (d. 1358 "Lunar"/1979): Professor of theology and philosophy at the University of Tehran and the Hawzah ʿIlmīyah of Qum who published extensively on a variety of issues related to Islām. He was a student of ʿAllāmah Ṭabāṭabāʾī and a close friend of ʿAllāmah Tihrānī. He was assassinated in Tehran in 1978.
23. Qāḍī, Ḥājj Mīrzā ʿAlī Āqā: (1285–1366 A.H./1867–1948) Scholar and professor of jurisprudence, ethics and *Ḥadīth* in Najaf and a prominent Sufi master who trained many outstanding students, including ʿAllāmah Ṭabāṭabāʾī and ʿAllāmah Tihrānī.
24. Qāḍī, Ḥājj Sayyid Ḥusayn Āqā: Shīʿī scholar who studied and taught in Najaf. He is the father of Ḥājj Mīrzā ʿAlī Āqā Qāḍī.
25. Qūchānī, Shaykh ʿAbbās: A teacher of ʿAllāmah Tihrānī in Najaf who introduced him to Ḥājj Sayyid Hāshim Ḥaddād.
26. Rūmī, Jalāl al-Dīn (604/672 A.H./1205/1273): The most important Persian Sufi thinker, metaphysician, and poet of all times. His Diwān of Shams-i Tabrīzī, and the Mathnawī have been translated into many languages and are widely known in the West.
27. Saʿdī, Shaykh Muṣliḥ al-Dīn: 610(15)–691/1213(19)–1292: Persian Sufi poet who wrote *Būstān* (Orchard, in prose) and *Gulistān* (Rose Garden, in poetry), and is one of the most eloquent and widely read Persian poets.
28. Salmān Fārsī: The Persian sage who left his homeland in search of the Blessed Prophet. He was captured and sold as a slave, but after much hardship met the Prophet, entered Islām, and became one of his close companions.
29. Shabastarī, Shaykh Maḥmūd (d. 842/1340): Educated in Tabrīz, he is considered one of the most eminent Sufi masters of Persia who was especially well-versed in Sufi symbolism. His Garden of Mysteries *(Gulshan-i Rāz)* has been widely read, commented upon, and translated into several languages including English.
30. Shīrāzī, Ḥājj Mīrzā Ḥasan: Known as *mīrzā-yi awwal,* he was the Supreme Source of Emulation *(marjaʿ-i taqlīd)* during the nineteenth

century and resided in Najaf. During the national protest movement in 1891–92 against granting a tobacco concession to the British, he issued the famous ruling *(fatwā)* prohibiting the consumption of tobacco.

31. Shīrāzī, Mīrzā Muhammad Taqī (d. 1339 A.H./1920): Known as *mīrzā-yi duwwum* and the author of *Dhakhirat al-ʿIbād* who proclaimed *jihād* in Iraq against the British dominance and played an important role in the independence movement of Iraq.
32. Shīrāzī, Ṣadr al-Dīn (Mullā Ṣadrā, 979–1050 A.H./1571–1641): The greatest philosopher of the Safavid period and the author of *Asfār-i Arbaʿah, Risāla-yi sih aṣl, Shawāhid al-Rubūbīyah fi manāhīj al-sulūkīyah,* and more than fifty other books.
33. Shūshtarī, Sayyid ʿAlī: Prominent ʿālim and the teacher of Shaykh Murtaḍā Anṣārī in ethics, who in turn taught Shūshtarī jurisprudence.
34. Tabāṭabāʾī, Muhammad Ḥasan: (1330–1391(?)/1906–1967). The younger brother of ʿAllāmah Ṭabāṭabāʾī, who received his education in Najaf and reached the rank of mujtahid a few years before his brother. He taught philosophy and ethics in Shīʿī learning centers in Tabrīz until his death.
35. Tihrānī, Āqā Buzurg: The author of *al-Dharīʿah,* the most authoritative biographical dictionary of the Shīʿī ʿulamā.
36. Tūsī, Khwājah Naṣīr al-Dīn Muhammad (598–672 A.H./1201–1274): Persian-Muslim philosopher, theologian, astronomer, and mathematician who was an adviser and minister to the Īlkhānid ruler Hulāgū, and played an important role in the spread of Shīʿism in Iran.
37. Zayn al-ʿĀbidīn Sajjād, ʿAlī ibn Ḥusayn: (d. 95 A.H./713) The grandson of Imām ʿAlī ibn Abī Ṭālib and the son of Ḥusayn ibn ʿAlī, he is the fourth Shīʿī Imām and is particularly known for compiling a collection of prayers known as the Scroll of Sajjād *(Ṣaḥīfah Sajjādīyah).* The book is also called the Psalms of the family of the Prophet (zabūr-i āl-i Muhammad).

INDEX

Printed in the United States
87856LV00005B/179/A

9 780791 452387